Chip Carving

GEOMETRIC PATTERNS TO DRAW AND CHIP OUT OF WOOD

CHIP CARVING

GEOMETRIC PATTERNS TO DRAW AND CHIP OUT OF WOOD

TATIANA BALDINA

~ Contents ~

INTRODUCTION

In this book, you will open the door to the world of chip carving. It is perhaps the simplest form of carving, but it can generate a huge variety of intricate and beautiful surface decoration. Whether you are exploring this world for the first time or you are already familiar with it, I will share my knowledge of the craft with you.

Any type of carving begins with the most basic patterns. Perfecting the technique of carving these simple elements is essential to beginning the study of chip carving. The main patterns are two-sided (ovals), three-sided (triangles) and four-sided (squares and rhombuses, with thin and wide lines) grooves of various sizes and depths.

If you see a complex chip carving design and think that you would never be able to carve it, try to break the complex pattern down into simple elements: you will see that the complex pattern is actually made up of many simple ones. Some people may say that it is hard to create something new and exciting with these simple shapes but, in my opinion, the charm of chip carving lies in this limitation. Who says that the triangles must have equal sides? Or that a line needs to be straight and not, for example, in the form of a rhombus?

These decisions spark creativity and the inspiration for fresh ideas.

Years after graduating from university, I have created almost 1,000 different chip carving patterns and have loved the process, but I have not always found it easy. To practise and get better, I set myself a challenge: to create a new pattern every day for a year. That is, I would create and draw one pattern a day, from beginning to end, drawing with capillary pens and filling in shadows. I still praise myself for this, since it gave me a huge step towards my dream of discovering new ways of approaching chip carving. Now this is much closer than it used to be. After several years of searching for something new in this kind of carving, I dived deep into the world of chip carving and opened up new facets. I continue to dive into it every day and I'm still not bored!

This book consists of 14 patterns that progress in difficulty, starting from a simple straight-wall chip and triangle and evolving through to more complex patterns. The templates for the designs can be found on page 168. On page 12, I explain how to transfer the templates for the patterns on to wood, but, if you want to draw a pattern on to the basswood board before carving it, each project offers full instructions on the drawing process before taking you step by step through the carving.

Although the two-dimensional patterns are decorative features in their own right, you could also turn them into three-dimensional objects. Chip carving designs can be used to decorate items such as large or small storage boxes or jewellery boxes, such as those shown in the gallery section (see page 172), or you can create beautiful coasters out of a simple board. There are no limits to what you can decorate with chip carving – this type of carving will look beautiful on whatever you choose!

You will also learn how to hold and work with skew knives. You may find this hard at first, but when you get the idea and learn the best knife positions for you then I am sure you will enjoy the process. In my opinion, the use of other tools, such as chisels, for this kind of carving makes it no longer chip carving but something else. It is a particular skill for a carver to create something beautiful, non-standard and soulful with just one or two knives. The wonderful thing is that by practising this craft you can discover something new and beautiful – and, most importantly, your own.

Welcome to the world of chip carving!

TOOLS AND MATERIALS

You will not need many tools and materials to start chip carving. A good skew knife and the means to keep it sharp are essential, along with drawing materials and a basswood board to carve.

BASSWOOD BOARD

In this book I have used basswood (*Tilia americana*) for all the projects. Also known as linden, this is the first kind of wood that I worked on when I was learning to carve. This wood is ideal for chip carving if it is properly dried because it is relatively soft and light, of a uniform structure, and easy to cut.

MECHANICAL PENCIL

To draw the patterns on to the basswood board, I use a 0.5–0.7mm mechanical pencil with an H or HB lead. This gives a thin and precise line. I use a polymer eraser for removing pencil lines, as it is neither too soft nor too hard.

COMPASS

You can use any compass as long as it allows you to draw both small circles (about 5mm in diameter) and large circles – the largest circle used in the projects in this book is almost 13cm in diameter.

RULER

I would suggest using a transparent ruler when ruling lines: the black guidelines on it stand out clearly on a white sheet of paper or on a light wood surface, and I find this helpful when drawing the patterns.

TYPES OF KNIFE

In Russia, we use skew knives or knife-hatchets for chip carving and these are what I have used throughout this book. There is another type of chip carving knife, used mostly in America and some parts of Europe, called an American knife.

There are many types of skew knife suitable for chip carving, from standard knife sizes to what we call in Russia knife-hatchets. The blade of the knife, up to the handle, can vary between about 2cm to 4cm in length, starting from the heel and not including the tip of the knife. The size of the blade can also vary.

Skew knives and knife-hatchets can either have a pronounced tip or not. The knife blade itself can be long or wide. The knife handles can have different shapes and sizes, from narrow to wide and round. I have worked with three brands of knives: Flexcut (I like their KN11 Flexcut skew knife); Forged Tool by Naumov (www.etsy.com/shop/forgedchisel), and Beaver Craft. Knives from Pfeil are also recommended, although I have not used one yet.

Basically, there are no bad knives; you just need to choose the one that is right for you. You may find you like another type of rigid-blade skew knife to carve patterns, as long as it is comfortable to hold and does not tire your hand while carving.

Above *A KN11 Flexcut skew knife on the left and an American chip carving knife on the right.*

Left *A knife-hatchet.*

TECHNIQUES

Here I describe the main techniques you will need to tackle the projects in this book, including sharpening knives, transferring a pattern to the board, and making stop cuts and undercuts.

SAFETY

These are the most basic safety precautions for working with carving knives.

1. Work at a table of comfortable height. There should be no foreign objects on the table, only the necessary tools: board, pencil, compass, eraser and ruler when drawing; board or other wooden blanks and knife when carving.

2. The workplace should be well lit, preferably from all sides. If it is daytime, then daylight should be enough if you sit by a window.

3. Remove the carved-out chips from the carving area as you work as they can cause damage to the edges of the work you have done.

4. Focus only on carving. For example, carve for 20–30 minutes, then take a break for 10 minutes to rest your hands and eyes. When you are tired and find it difficult to focus only on carving, your chances of cutting yourself or breaking the carving are higher.

5. Work only with a sharp knife. Remember that you can cut yourself either by not adhering to the safety precautions, not using your supporting hand when carving, or when working with a dull knife.

6. Your supporting hand should not be in the way of the knife's movement and, in general, should be well away from the carving process. While working with a skew knife, the supporting hand both holds the board and participates in carving.

The supporting hand should be kept away from the direction of the knife's movement while carving to avoid cutting yourself.

SHARPENING A KNIFE

Get into the habit of sharpening your knife regularly, especially before you start work on a new pattern (or a part of a pattern that requires very sharp multi-level patterns), as this will help to give you consistent results.

My preferred sharpening method is to use abrasive or sandpaper films or strips. I stick these along the edge of a sheet of glass that has had the sharp edge removed **1**. The sandpaper films I use range from 600 or 2000 to 6000 grit. The very first sandpaper I use depends on the condition of my knife at the moment I am going to sharpen it. The highest grit I use instead of a leather strip; I use this for polishing. The lower the grit of a film, the fewer movements you make when sharpening; the higher its grit, the more movements you make. You make roughly three or four knife movements on each side of the knife when sharpening on 2000 grit; five or six movements on 3000 grit; and seven or eight movements on 6000 grit.

For me, skew blades are best sharpened while oriented to run in a straight line **2**. In my opinion, this works best because it is easier to hold at a constant angle, and leads to a more highly polished cutting surface before using higher-grit sandpaper and polishing. Sharpening along the surface of the films tends to result in a rounded cutting edge,

even if I try to hold a constant angle **3**. A strip of leather (also known as a strop) can be used along with some honing paste to polish the surface of the bevel.

After sharpening the blade, rinse it with water and wipe dry. And after you have finished working with the knife, wipe it gently (so as not to cut yourself) with a dry rag. Put a block of solid foam on the cutting edge to protect it **4** and wrap the tool in a case roll or store it in a special box **5**.

1 Abrasive strips stuck onto a sheet of glass.

2 This shows the best method I have found to sharpen a straight-edge skewed blade using abrasive films.

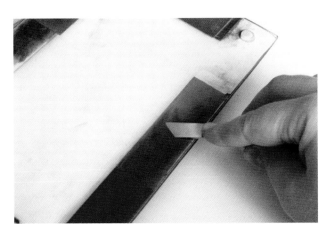

3 This shows how you can sharpen a knife along the surface of the films; however, every time I use this method I obtain a rounded cutting edge even if I try to hold a constant angle.

4 Solid foam on the cutting edge protects the blade.

5 Keep the knife in a special box for tools.

TRANSFERRING THE PATTERN TO THE BASSWOOD BOARD

Before you can start drawing the patterns, you need to prepare the basswood board. If you are a beginner, I would advise you to transfer the patterns with carbon paper (the templates for the designs in this book can be found on page 168). If you already have some experience, you can try drawing the patterns by hand, following the steps described for each project in this book.

To transfer a pattern, first scan or photocopy the template from the book (see pages 168–171). Print out the pattern if you have scanned it.

Next, lay the carbon paper, ink-coated side down, on to the board where the pattern should go **1**. Place the printed pattern on top of the carbon paper, then fasten these sheets to the board with masking tape so that they do not move **2**.

Trace over the pattern using an HB pencil (a standard one, not a mechanical one) or a ball-point pen that has run out of ink. Be sure to press hard enough with the pencil or pen to transfer the design on to the wood through the layers of paper **3**. When you are sure that all the details have been transferred, remove the tape and sheets **4**.

1 The carbon paper in place on the wood, ink side down.

2 Fasten the sheets to the board with masking tape.

3 Here I used a ball-point pen that has run out of ink to transfer the design on to the wood.

4 Remove the tape and sheets when all of the design has been transferred.

HOLDING A SKEW KNIFE

When carving, there are two directions of movement of a skew knife – towards yourself and away from yourself. The carving motion of the knife towards yourself is when the heel of the knife is turned towards you **1**. The carving motion of the knife away from yourself is when the heel of the knife is turned away from you **2**.

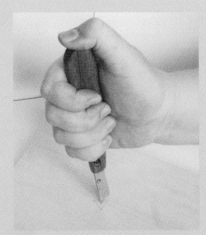

1 The heel of the knife turned towards you.

2 The heel of the knife turned away from you.

STOP CUTS

Stop cuts are the cuts made in the places where the facets of the chips connect with each other, starting from the deepest part of the chip. When you take the first steps in carving and practise carving simple patterns again and again, stop cuts not only show you where to stop undercutting one side or the other of any chip, but also set the depth of the chip (I talk about this more during the carving process of the Triangles pattern; see page 28).

Before you start to carve you need to make stop cuts, not only to feel the angle at which the knife tilts when undercutting the chips – triangles, ovals and

so on – but so you don't go beyond the previously made stop cuts first. You also need to be aware of 'invisible' stop cuts: the angle at which the knife tilts when undercutting these chips is different; therefore, it takes some time for the muscle memory to remember these tilts and the angle of undercutting.

Stop cuts are made perpendicular to the surface of the wood, starting from the deepest point of the chip. Place the knife where the deepest point will be **1**. Push the knife deep into the wood **2**, then lower the heel to the base **3**. These steps are then repeated on the other stop cut lines.

1 Knife set at the deepest point.

2 Push the knife deep into the wood.

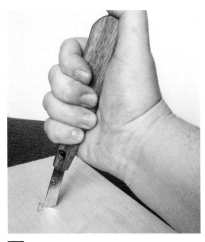

3 Lower the heel to the base.

UNDERCUTTING

Undercutting refers to the repetitive motion of a knife at one angle on all sides of any chip in order to completely remove it.

To make an undercut, hold the knife with four fingers at a comfortable distance from the knife blade. Let your thumb lie on the knife handle. Set the undercutting angle at 45 degrees. In the picture, I demonstrate the undercutting technique using the example of a triangle. Hold the board with your second hand, and put the thumb of your supporting hand on the back edge of the blade to push the knife **1**.

Now undercut the second side of a triangle, but working away from you **2**. This grip is more complicated than the first one. At the top of the handle, place the thumb, forefinger and middle finger, with the thumb and forefinger together and the middle finger a bit further away, closer to the blade of the knife **3**. At the bottom of the handle, the ring finger supports the knife **4** and the little finger is at a comfortable distance from the carved pattern **5**. This can regulate the angle at which the knife is tilted in relation to the carved pattern **6**. In this image I am undercutting the base of a triangle by cutting towards myself **7**.

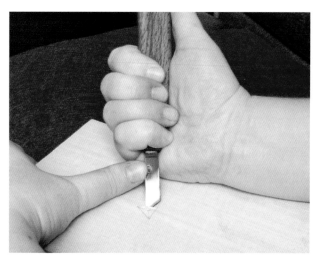

1 Holding the board with the second hand, and push the knife on the back edge with the thumb.

2 Undercutting the second side of a triangle in the position away from you.

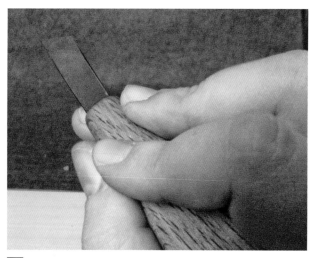

3 Holding the knife to undercut the side in the position away from you – view from above.

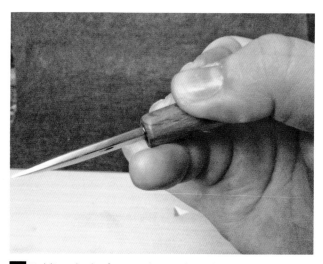

4 Holding the knife to undercut the side in the position away from you – position of the ring finger.

5 Undercutting the side away from you – little finger held out of the way.

6 Regulating the angle at which the knife is tilted.

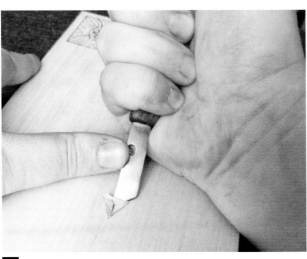

7 Undercutting the base of a triangle towards yourself.

MANY WOODCARVERS SAY THAT IT IS NECESSARY TO GRIND THE SURFACE OF THE WOOD BEFORE YOU START CARVING. I DO NOT AGREE, SINCE THE KNIFE WILL BECOME DULL MUCH FASTER THAN IF THE SURFACE OF THE WOOD IS NOT POLISHED BEFORE CARVING.

1 Undercutting where the sides are not clearly along or against the grain.

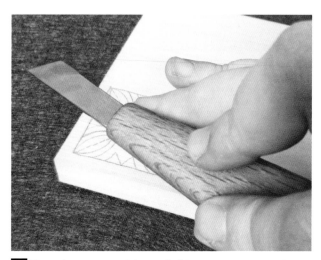

2 To undercut a straight-wall chip, use your second hand to steady the knife.

3 Undercutting a straight-wall chip away from you.

STRAIGHT-WALL CHIPS

A straight-wall chip is the simplest pattern in chip carving. It can be either an equilateral triangle (where all three sides are equal) or an isosceles triangle (where two of the sides are equal). No stop cuts are needed to carve this. Accordingly, there is no need to keep the knife at the same angle while undercutting the sides in a simple triangle to remove the chip, which has three facets, or when a triangle is divided into three parts or three straight-wall chips.

Undercutting a straight-wall chip towards yourself

To undercut a straight-wall chip towards yourself, when the sides are not clearly located along the grain or against the grain, you need to undercut very carefully. To do this, when the sides are undercut at an angle of almost 90 degrees, hold the knife in your hand, away from the blade, so that the blade is laid as close as possible to the surface of the wood. Next, hold the board with the free fingers of your second hand and place the thumb of this supporting hand on the knife's back edge. This will act as a kind of counterweight: the hand with the knife moves forwards and slightly to the left, as if grabbing the side along which the tip moves and, accordingly, inside the wood if there is no counterweight. Instead we need the knife to move parallel to the side to which it is going **1**.

Undercutting a straight-wall chip away from yourself

The last technique involves undercutting a straight-wall chip away from yourself. If you try to cut it like a triangle, by moving away from you, you will not be able to lay the knife blade close to the surface of the wood. Hold your fingers away from the blade. The thumb and forefinger should be together, the middle finger a little further from them and closer to the blade of the knife, and the ring finger will be next to the little finger **2**. In this case, it will be possible to put the knife blade on the surface of the wood and carve the chip **3**.

CARVING AT DIFFERENT ANGLES

Carving of all chips can be done at any angle you want. However, there are some basic angles for undercutting, when this or that chip looks best on the surface of the wood:

For undercutting two sides of a straight-wall chip, you need to make a cut at an angle of almost 90 degrees to the surface of the wood.

MULTI-LEVEL CARVING

In the instructions for the patterns, I sometimes refer to multi-level carving. This is a type of carving when smaller straight-wall chips are carved inside bigger straight-wall chips. These smaller and bigger chips can be in the form of isosceles triangles but also other forms and shapes too.

An angle of almost 60 degrees.

An angle of almost 90 degrees.

FINISHING

Rather than hiding the work you have done with thick layers of stain and varnish, finishing should reveal the carving and enhance its beauty, which is what Danish oil does. You can buy Danish oil with or without an added stain. It can be applied both with a synthetic brush (when applying oil on carving) or with a soft rag (when applying oil to a smooth wood surface).

First layer: Apply Danish oil without any stain. This layer of oil prepares the wood grain and carved surface for the next layers of oil with any kind of tone (light or dark ones) and doesn't let that tone of oil go deep into the grain. Before adding the next layer of oil, brush the carved surface with a clean soft toothbrush. I don't like using sandpaper, because one of the most important aspects in chip carving is to keep the edges of the carving sharp.

Second layer: Apply a layer of Danish oil with a stain. Third layer: Apply another layer of Danish oil with a stain. Fourth layer: Apply a layer of Danish oil without any stain.

A piece finished with Danish oil.

YOU DON'T HAVE TO USE OIL WITH A STAIN STRAIGHT FROM THE JAR. IF YOU DON'T LIKE THE SHADE, YOU CAN MIX DIFFERENT STAINS TOGETHER IN A RATIO YOU PREFER. USE A SCRAP OF WOOD TO PRACTISE ON BEFORE APPLYING TO YOUR FINISHED PIECE.

PRACTICE BOARD SAMPLER

Practice is something you need for any craft if you want to do it well. For chip carving, there are at least three kinds of practice boards with different levels of difficulty: carving the patterns against the grain, along the grain, and in different directions. Practising on patterns that go against the grain is the best way for beginners to start chip carving. My practice board has 25 lines (front and back) with four different levels of difficulty, beginning with linear geometric or repeat patterns.

DRAWING THE PATTERNS

Transfer the templates on page 168 on to the basswood board following the instructions on page 12.

CARVING THE FIRST SIDE OF THE BOARD

Before you start to carve, place your practice board on to a flat rigid surface with a non-slip mat beneath if you have one. To produce clean and consistent cuts, you need to position your knife in exactly the same manner each time you make a similar cut in the pattern.

TOOLS AND MATERIALS

- BASSWOOD BOARD, 250MM LONG X 150MM WIDE X 15MM THICK

- SKEW KNIFE

- SANDPAPER OR LEATHER STRIPS FOR SHARPENING

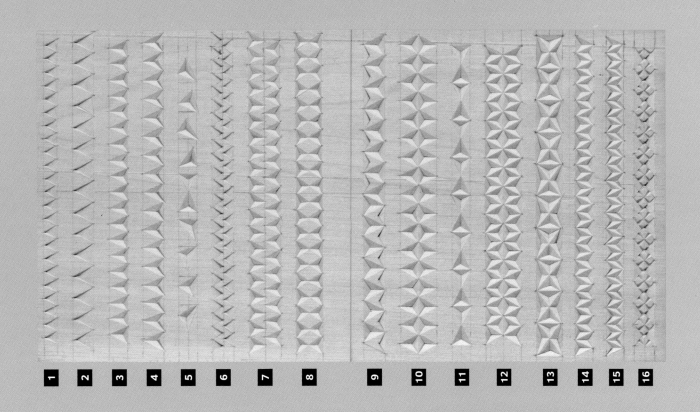

| 1 | 2 | 3 | 4 | 5 | 6 | 7 | 8 | 9 | 10 | 11 | 12 | 13 | 14 | 15 | 16 |

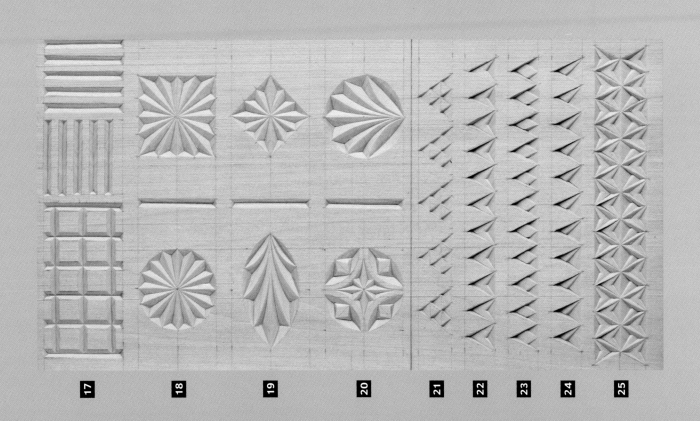

| 17 | 18 | 19 | 20 | 21 | 22 | 23 | 24 | 25 |

Lines 1 and 2: For this exercise, you need to hold the knife directly above the first side of the chip at about 90 degrees to the surface, then gently push the tip of the blade deep to the top of the triangle, where the facets meet **1**. Then, without removing the knife from the wood, lower the heel of the knife to the base of the triangle, to the third side of it, without applying any pressure **2**. Try to capture the feel of the blade as it pierces the wood and the movement of the technique. Now repeat those steps on the other long side of the triangle.

Turn the board away from you (around 35–45 degrees) so that you can lay the knife blade low to the surface of the wood along the bottom of the triangle and push the knife towards the top of the triangle where the sides intersect at the top **3**. Again, try to remember the feel of the technique so you can reproduce it on the following chip. Continue across the board, making adjustments as necessary while working towards creating a consistent pattern.

Line 2 is a bigger version of this straight-wall chip. The carving technique is exactly the same, so just repeat all the steps and work towards creating a consistent pattern from making a series of identical cuts in both depth and alignment.

Line 3: The simple triangle is a more complex chip pattern than the previous ones. Hold the

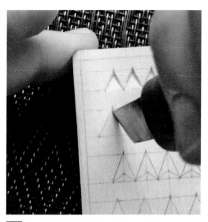

1 Hold the knife firmly at about 90 degrees to the surface of the board. Then push the knife tip deep into the wood.

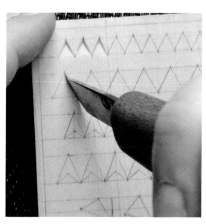

2 Lower the heel of the knife blade along the pencil line to the base of the triangle.

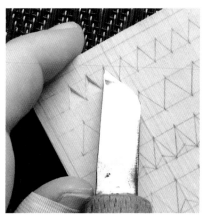

3 Push the knife towards the intersecting corner of the straight-wall sides to remove the chip.

4 Put the heel of the blade at the centre of the triangle and lower it along the line to the top of the chip.

5 Rotate the board and complete the two remaining stop cuts.

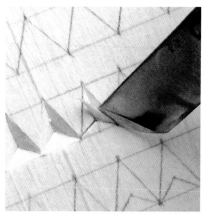

6 Place the knife at the edge of the triangle at 45 degrees to undercut the first chip.

7 Rotate the board and undercut the second chip.

8 Rotate the board a second time and undercut the third side. The chip will pop out.

knife firmly at 90 degrees to the surface of the board. Then push the knife tip deep into the wood at the centre of the chip. Then, gradually removing the pressure, lower the heel of the knife to the top of the triangle **4**. Repeat this technique for the remaining two stop cuts **5**. Then, angling the knife at 45 degrees, work around the edge of the triangle to remove the chips one at a time **6**, **7**, **8**. For consistent results, it is important to maintain the same angle for all the angled cuts so that the pattern appears uniform on all sides. I recommend you make the stop cuts while you are learning to chip carve.

When you are comfortable with this technique, you can try removing the waste by just using angled cuts. If you have been holding the knife correctly, a single chip will pop out. However, there are times when this doesn't happen, so you will have to repeat the cuts or make stop cuts to sever the wood fibres at the meeting points.

9 Insert the blade to cut along a straight line.

10 Removing a chip that meets at the top of the triangle.

Line 4: Undercut the sides of the triangles at an angle of 45 degrees. Then, to remove the sides, cut them by pushing the knife tip into the wood, in the places where the stop cut lines of the non-removed bases are, at an angle of almost 90 degrees to the surface of the sides.

Line 5: Undercut the sides of the triangles that go in different directions at 45 degrees.

Line 6: The next pattern to carve is the 'snake made of straight-wall chips', as it translates from Russian. To carve this pattern, repeat all the steps made when carving a small straight-wall chip **9**, **10**.

Lines 7 and 8: Undercut the sides and the bases of the triangles at 45 degrees.

Line 9: Cut the sides of the small straight-wall chips at an angle of 90 degrees, and, by putting the cutting edge of the knife on to the surface of the wood, push the knife towards the intersecting corner to remove the chip; undercut the sides and the bases of the triangles at a 45-degree angle.

Line 10: Undercut the sides and the bases of the triangles at a 45-degree angle.

Line 11: The pattern from this section is a chain of isosceles triangles that are connected to each other. As you can see, this pattern runs along the grain, so requires a different carving technique. This is good preparation for the complex pattern we will be carving next.

Make stop cuts inside every triangle in the pattern **11**. When carving a chip that goes along the grain, the first cut you make is the 'base' cut, or the third cut you were making when you carved the first triangle on the board that ran across the grain. After the first cut is done, turn the board and make the next cuts **12**.

Always lead the knife along the grain, as shown in the photos, otherwise you could break the chip and the angles, or you could crush the wood fibres inside the triangles. This leaves a rough surface on the inside faces of the pattern that will be hard to correct **13**, **14**, **15**.

Lines 12, 13 and 14: Undercut the sides and the bases of the triangles at an angle of 45 degrees.

Line 15: Undercut the sides of the triangles at an angle of 45 degrees. Then, to remove the sides, cut them by pushing the knife tip into the wood, in the places where the stop cut lines of the non-removed bases are, at an angle of almost 90 degrees to the surface of the sides.

11 Complete the stop cuts inside the triangle, starting with the long line.

12 Now complete the two shorter stop cuts.

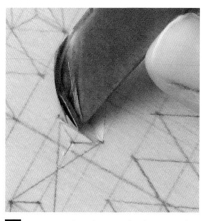

13 Remove the chip at the base with angles cut at 45 degrees.

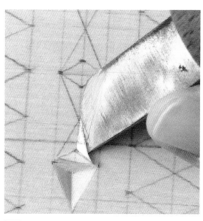

14 Now remove the second chip with another angled cut.

Line 16: Cut the sides of the straight-wall chips around the rhombuses at an angle of 90 degrees. By putting the cutting edge of the knife on to the surface of the wood, push the knife towards the intersecting corner to remove the chip; then remove the chips inside the rhombuses at an angle of 60 degrees.

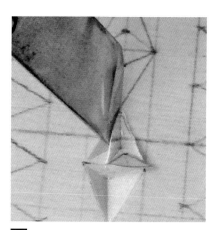

15 Remove the third chip with another angled cut to complete the shape.

16 Creating the stop cuts first helps to identify the high and low spots in the design.

17 Try to avoid cutting the stop cuts right up to the centre of the pattern for now.

18 This complete set of stop cuts clearly outlines the 16 three-corner chips around the edge.

19 Use the tip of the knife to carve the first chip at the perimeter of the pattern.

CARVING THE SECOND SIDE OF THE BOARD

Line 17: Undercut the long and short sides of the long four-sided chips at an angle of 60 degrees.

Line 18: Undercut the sides of the triangles inside the square at 45 degrees; and undercut the long and short sides of the long four-sided chips at 60 degrees.

The circle has 16 three-corner chips. This is a complex pattern and may be tricky to carve because there are chips that go along the grain, across the grain and at various angles diagonal to the run of grain. The chips of this pattern also connect with each other, so you need to have good control of your knife.

I prefer to start carving this pattern from the chips that go along the grain. To me, it seems easier to control carving the next chips when these ones are done. First, start by making the stop cuts inside every chip: raise the knife right above the centre where the stop cuts meet, then stick the very tip of the knife into it at 90 degrees to the wood surface. Gently drag the tip of the blade along the line, stopping short of the centre. Repeat this for all of the stop cuts **16**, **17**, **18**.

Start carving the pattern from one of the four chips that go along the grain, and make the base cut first **19**. Then, pushing the knife deep to the central point where all the stop cuts inside the triangle meet, lead the knife to the centre of the pattern using

TAKE ONE STEP BACK EVERY DAY

Taking a step back in your learning is not regressive; it does not involve giving up on your plans, but rather repeating the steps you have already made and consolidating new knowledge. Without repetition, there is no progression. In other words, if you start with something brand new every day, you will be building on fragile foundations. For example, when I receive an order for a practice board where one board needs to be completely carved, it is like returning to when I learned to carve for the very first time. I am carving the simplest patterns all over again, but with a new, deeper understanding.

the tip or heel of the knife . Turn the knife in your hand and repeat the actions to complete the chip 21. Continue to carve the chips to one and then to the other side of the carved chip following the grain of the wood, and go right to the centre of the pattern. Then carve another side of the pattern, starting from the chip that goes along the grain 22. Finish carving all the chips using the method used on the other side to complete the pattern 23.

Line 19: Undercut the sides of the triangles inside the oval and the rhombus at an angle of 45 degrees; then undercut the long and short sides of the long four-sided chips at 60 degrees.

Line 20: Undercut the sides and the bases of the triangles inside the circle at 45 degrees and the sides of the ovals at 60 degrees. Undercut the long and short sides of the long four-sided chips at 60 degrees; undercut the sides of the triangles inside the central rhombus of the circle at 45 degrees and the sides of the triangles without bases inside the ovals at 45 degrees. To remove the sides, cut them by pushing the knife tip into the wood, in the places where the stop cut lines of the non-removed bases are, at almost 90 degrees to the surface of the sides.

Line 21: Cut the sides of the small straight-wall chips at an angle of 90 degrees, and, by putting the cutting edge of the knife onto the surface, push the knife towards the intersecting corner to remove the chip.

20 Push the knife deep into the centre of the chip. Then gently lead it to the centre of the pattern.

21 Rotate the board and make the third cut.

22 Cutting along the grain away from the centre of the pattern.

23 A finished circle with 16 three-corner chips completely carved.

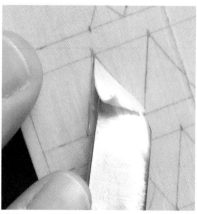

24 Make stop cuts and remove a regular straight-wall chip.

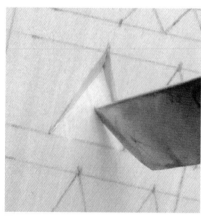

25 Place the tip of the knife in the centre of the big chip area.

26 Make two stop cuts from the centre to the base of the triangle.

27 Lower the knife and push it towards the centre point.

28 A smaller chip will break loose and complete the pattern.

Line 22: The last section is for multi-level carving. I have chosen one of the basic patterns for this: it is not as complex as it might seem at first glance.

The technique for carving this pattern is the same as you used for the small and bigger straight-wall chips. By now you should be able to accomplish them quite quickly with consistent results. Raise the knife right above the first side of the chip, then push the tip of the knife deep to the top of the triangle, where the facets meet, at almost 90 degrees. Then, without removing the knife from the wood, lower the heel of the knife to the base of the chip, reducing pressure as you go until you are applying no pressure at all. Then repeat on the other side **24**.

Now turn the board away from you (35–45 degrees) so you can lay the blade low to the wood along the third side of the chip (the short side of your isosceles triangle), and push the knife towards the intersecting corner of the straight-wall sides (the apex of the triangle). To carve the smaller chip inside this chip, stab the knife at almost 90 degrees – not to the surface of the board this time, but to the surface on the big chip instead **25**. Repeat all the steps you made on the straight-wall chips to remove a smaller chip **26**, **27**, **28**.

Line 23: Cut the sides of the multi-level chip at almost 90 degrees and, by putting the cutting edge of the knife onto the surface, push the knife towards the intersecting corner to remove the chip. Then carve two smaller straight-wall chips inside this one so that they form a rhombus inside it.

Line 24: Cut the sides of the multi-level chip at almost 90 degrees and, by putting the cutting edge of the knife onto the surface, push the knife towards the intersecting corner to remove the chip. Then carve a smaller straight-wall chip/scalene triangle (a triangle with three unequal sides) inside this one, starting to undercut it from the right side, stepping 2–3mm from the base of the big chip. Inside the chips, starting from the central one, carve two smaller chips/scalene triangles inside the big one, by repeating all the previous steps.

Line 25: First, carve the inner chips or the straight-wall chips that are connected by bases to each other. Cut the sides of the chips at almost 90 degrees and, by putting the cutting edge of the knife on to the surface of the wood, push the knife towards the intersecting corner to remove the chips. Then carve the smaller chip/isosceles triangle inside the top chip and the scalene triangle inside the bottom chip. Then carve the chips around these ones, and the smaller chips/isosceles triangles inside them.

THE
PATTERNS

TRIANGLES

The first pattern consists of the simplest triangles: both ones that are self-contained and those that are connected by bases to each other.

TOOLS AND MATERIALS

- BASSWOOD BOARD (AT LEAST 100–120MM SQUARE AND 15MM THICK)

- 0.5MM MECHANICAL PENCIL WITH H OR HB LEAD

- RULER

- COMPASS

- SKEW KNIFE

- SANDPAPER OR LEATHER STRIPS FOR SHARPENING

- LONG NAIL AND HAMMER

DRAWING PROCESS

If you would prefer to transfer this pattern to the basswood board, the template is on page 169, and guidelines on page 12. Otherwise, if you prefer to draw the pattern directly on to the basswood board, follow the instructions below.

First draw a square with sides that are 4cm long. Then draw two perpendicular lines that intersect at the centre and two diagonal lines that connect the opposite corners of the square **1**. Next, prepare a circle for the central main pattern: mark a dot 1.5cm from the central point of the square on any of the perpendicular lines **2**. This is the radius of the circle. Draw this circle using a compass **3**. Keep the radius at 15mm and mark dots on the diagonal lines: place the compass at those two dots where the circle intersects the perpendicular vertical line above and below, and draw short lines to the right and left from that point **4**. Putting the compass on these dots, draw curved lines inside each quarter of the circle **5**.

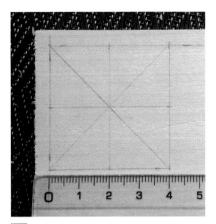

1 Draw a square with sides that are 4cm long, then draw two perpendicular and two diagonal lines.

2 Measure 1.5cm from the central point of the square.

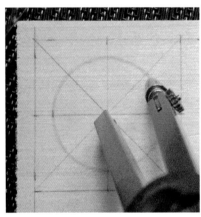

3 Using a compass, draw a circle with a 1.5cm radius.

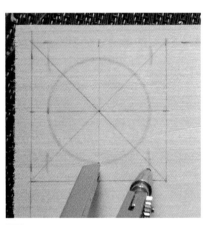

4 Still using a 1.5cm radius, place the compass point where the circle intersects the vertical line and draw short lines on the diagonal lines.

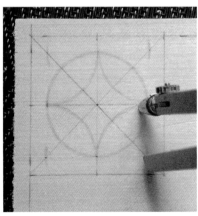

5 Place a compass on the prepared short lines, and draw curved lines inside the circle.

6 Mark a dot 9mm from the centre.

7 Draw the thickness of the sharp ovals and separate them from the central pattern.

8 Draw a square at the centre of the pattern.

Next, add thickness to the resulting curved lines. Mark a dot 9mm from the centre of the square **6**, and, by placing the compass on the dots on the diagonal lines that were marked to draw the ovals, draw a curved line **7**. Now draw a small square in the centre of the pattern: simply connect those points where the diagonal lines intersect the inner curved line of the ovals **8**.

The central pattern is ready. You now need to draw the patterns in the corners of the square and also a line for hammering. Then you need to draw the lines inside each pattern for stop cuts.

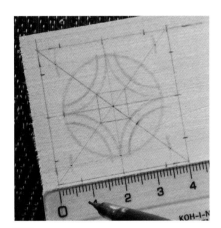

9 Measure 7mm from each corner – down, up, right, left – and mark dots on the vertical and horizontal sides of the main square.

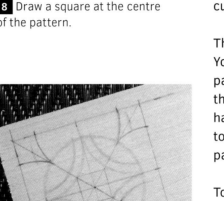

10 Connect the dots with the places where the circle crosses the diagonal lines.

To draw the patterns in the corners of the square, measure 7mm from each corner – down, up, right, left – and mark dots on the vertical and horizontal sides of the main square **9**. Then draw curved lines by hand that connect the prepared points together where the circle intersects the diagonal lines **10**.

Next, put a dot on any of the diagonal or perpendicular lines 1.8cm from the centre of the square, or 3mm from the line of the circle **11**. With a compass, draw curved lines that do not connect with each other in places where there are patterns in the corners **12**.

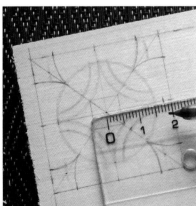

11 Measure 1.8cm from the centre.

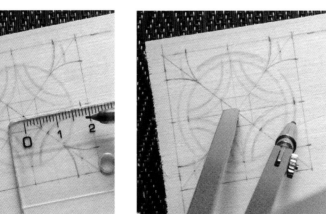

12 Draw curved lines for hammering using a compass.

Then, by placing the compass on those dots where curved lines intersect the perpendicular lines, draw short lines 2–3mm from the outer lines of the corner patterns to indicate where the hammering will end **13**.

Now start drawing lines for stop cuts. Start with the patterns in the corners: connect the dots of the small rhombuses on the horizontal and vertical lines of the main square. The resulting lines will be perpendicular to the main diagonal lines that are partially in the corner patterns and that are also bases where two triangles are connected into one rhombus **14**. Mark dots 2mm to the right and left of the diagonal line **15**, then connect them to the points of the common base of the triangles **16**.

Now turn to the central pattern. Divide in half those diagonal lines that are partially in the outer shapes of the circle (sharp ovals) **17**. Then connect the tops of the sharp ovals to these dots **18**.

13 Separate the curved lines from the rhombuses in the corners of the square.

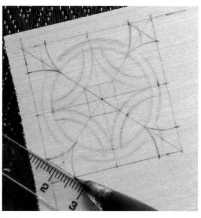

14 Draw the lines for stop cuts inside each rhombus.

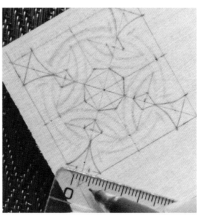

15 Mark a dot 2mm from the diagonal lines to the left and right inside each rhombus.

16 Connect the dots with the base.

17 Divide the widest place of the ovals in half.

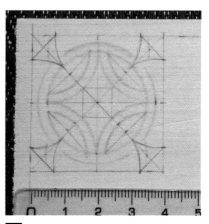

18 Connect the dot with the tops of the ovals.

19 Mark dots 2.5mm on the left and right of the diagonal line.

20 Connect the dots with the triangles' bases.

On the resulting lines, mark a dot 2.5mm from the common base of future triangles/the diagonal line of the main square **19**. Connect it to the base of the triangles; namely, at those dots where the diagonal line passes through the middle of the sharp oval **20**.

Where there are four inner individual triangles, mark dots 2mm from the sides of the inner square **21**, and connect them to their corners **22**.

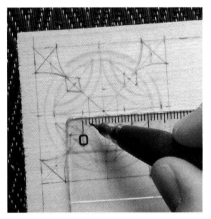

21 Mark dots 2mm from the central square on the vertical and horizontal perpendicular lines.

22 Connect the dots with the triangles' bases.

FAKE IT TILL YOU MAKE IT

I had a revelation while teaching a student to carve triangles. Nothing was working as it should; every time, the knife went beyond the lines of the stop cuts. Then I thought, what if my student could apply the phrase 'fake it till you make it' to carving these simple triangles? I said, 'Let's imagine that when you undercut the first facet, the other two do not exist. It's as if the task is to carve one chip, as if this is one straight-wall chip, but just carving it at a different angle, that's all.' Accordingly, if those two facets do not exist, then the knife will no longer try to go beyond the lines of the stop cuts. And, very slowly, my student started to get it right. Perhaps this idea will help you with carving any pattern, both those with additional stop cuts, and those without.

CARVING PROCESS

First, make stop cuts inside all the triangles of the pattern **23**. The central four triangles are the simplest in this pattern, as they are isolated and not connected to other patterns and triangles. Therefore, it is best to start with them, or rather, with the two whose sides go along the grain. Place the knife at the edge of the triangle at 45 degrees to undercut the first chip. Try to keep the blade of the knife parallel to the stop cut at the base of the triangle **24**. Rotate the board and undercut the second facet **25**. Rotate the board a second time and undercut the third side **26**. If the chip does not pop out, repeat the cuts at the same angle on all the sides of the triangle. Then carve the triangle on the opposite side, following the same steps.

Now carve those triangles whose bases go along the grain. Undercut the base of the first upper triangle (in my case, the knife went smoothly along the grain when the undercut was made away from me) **27**. Then carve its sides, keeping your knife at 45 degrees **28**.

23 Make stop cuts inside all the triangles of the pattern.

24 Place the knife at the edge of the triangle at 45 degrees to undercut the first chip.

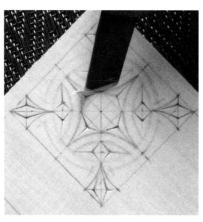

25 Rotate the board and undercut the second facet.

26 Rotate the board a second time and undercut the base of the triangle.

27 Undercut the base of the first upper triangle, which goes along the grain – it might be towards you or away from you.

28 Remove the sides of the triangles at a 45-degree angle.

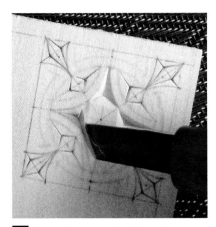

29 Carve the opposite triangle, starting from the base, then carve its sides.

30 The central individual triangles are completely carved out.

Now carve the opposite triangle, also starting from the base. On this triangle, the base is already undercutting towards you **29**. Carve out the central individual triangles **30**.

Now start working on the triangles inside the sharp ovals. These triangles are connected to each other by bases. Therefore, it is preferable to start carving from the base, following the grain direction, and then carve the sides **31**, **32**, **33**, **34**.

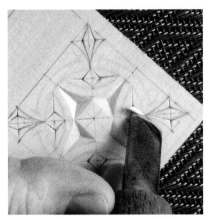

31 Start carving the first triangle from the base, following the direction of the grain.

32 Then carve the sides, holding the knife at a 45-degree angle.

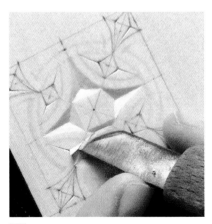

33 Start carving the second triangle inside the oval, also from the base.

34 The two triangles connected by the bases inside one oval are carved.

When the triangles in one oval are finished, carve the triangles in the other three ovals 35.

Now carve the triangles in the corners of the square, which are also connected by bases to each other. Start carving the sides exactly where the common bases are 36. Carve out one rhombus at a time 37 and then the remaining ones 38. Follow my theory of carving the opposite sides that go along the grain (see box), since there are such sides here.

The last stage is to hammer a circle in a broken line around the central pattern. For this, you need a long nail and a hammer 39. First, put a nail in those places on the perpendicular lines where the incomplete circle intersects them, and hit the hammer once to make a small hole 40.

35 Finish carving the next triangles in the other ovals.

36 Start carving the sides of the triangles where the common bases go.

37 Carve out one rhombus at a time.

38 Finish carving the rest of the rhombuses.

39 A long nail and a hammer.

40 Hammer a nail once in the places on the perpendicular lines where the incomplete circle intersects them.

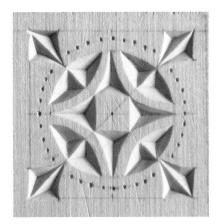

Then hammer holes to the right and left of these dots, making four holes in each segment by eye, until the circle is complete **41**.

The carving is now complete **42**.

41 Then, to the right and left of the dots, make four hammer blows on the nail.

42 The completely carved pattern.

CARVING ALONG THE GRAIN

When carving along the grain, the most important thing is what your hand feels while carving: either it feels that the undercut will not go smoothly along the grain (in which case you need to change the direction of movement of your knife or the grip in your hand), or the undercut goes smoothly, like cutting butter, in which case nothing needs to be changed.

It is impossible to know in advance how you will need to hold the knife – whether towards you or away from you. Every time, when moving your knife along the grain, you need to try carefully until the undercut goes easily, without breaking

the grain. In my theory – proven many times in practice – carving chips along the grain goes like this: if on one side, for example, you undercut holding the knife towards you (only when the knife goes easily through the grain without breaking it), then the other side will need to be undercut away from you. Therefore, you will not need to check again how to undercut the other side when you have already undercut one side (this applies to patterns such as four-sided long chips that go along the grain; two triangles connected with the bases that go along the grain, and so on).

PETALS

The chips in this pattern are not too difficult to carve, but you will notice the difference when carving relatively large chips like the ovals and the very thin cuts in the centre of the pattern.

TOOLS AND MATERIALS

- BASSWOOD BOARD (AT LEAST 100–120MM SQUARE AND 15MM THICK)

- 0.5MM MECHANICAL PENCIL WITH H OR HB LEAD

- RULER

- COMPASS

- SKEW KNIFE

- SANDPAPER OR LEATHER STRIPS FOR SHARPENING

DRAWING PROCESS

If you would prefer to transfer this pattern to the basswood board, the template is on page 169, and guidelines on page 12. Otherwise, to draw the pattern directly on to the board, follow these instructions.

First draw a square with the sides that are 4cm long. Draw two perpendicular lines that intersect at the centre and two diagonal lines that connect the opposite corners of the square **1**. Next, prepare two circles for the central pattern. First, mark a dot 1cm from the centre **2**. Draw a circle using a compass **3**. Divide the radius of the resulting circle in half, mark a dot **4** and draw another circle **5**.

Mark dots 7.5mm on the right and left of those dots through which the perpendicular lines pass, and divide the sides of the main square in half **6**. Next, place a compass on one of the dots, and draw a curved line starting from the corner of the square to the dot on the diagonal line where the outer square intersects it (you get only one curved line from one dot) **7**. Repeat these steps for the remaining dots **8**.

Mark a dot 2mm from the sides of the resulting sharp ovals **9**, and draw curved lines with a compass **10**. Now prepare triangles for straight-wall chips: put the compass on one of the dots on the sides of the main square and draw short lines starting from the dots that go on

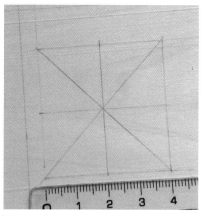

1 Draw a square with sides that are 4cm long, then draw two perpendicular and two diagonal lines.

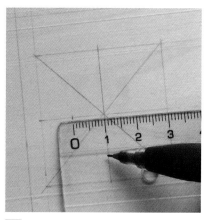

2 Measure 1cm to draw a circle inside the square.

3 Using a compass, draw a circle with a 1cm radius.

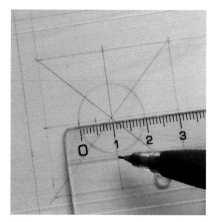

4 Divide the radius of the circle in half.

5 Using a compass, draw another circle inside the first one.

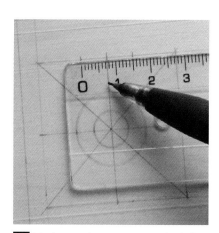

6 Mark two dots 7.5mm to the left and right from the points where the vertical perpendicular line crosses the top side of the square.

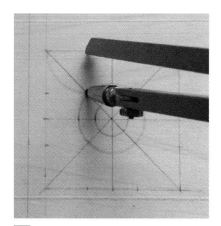

7 Put the compass on the first dot, then draw a curved line.

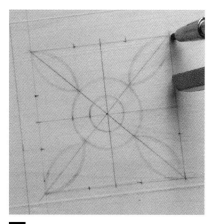

8 Put the compass on each dot in turn and draw the remaining curved lines.

the side perpendicularly to the side where the compass is **11**.

Measure 5.5–6mm from the sides of the main square, and mark a dot or short line on one of the resulting sides of the future straight-wall chip **12**. Or, to save time, mark a dot on one of the lines, and then, using a compass, draw short lines on all the other ones **13**. Now connect the resulting dots with those that divide the sides of the main square in half **14**.

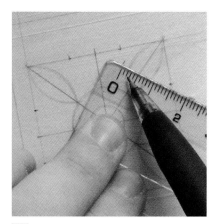

9 Mark a dot 2mm from the side of the oval.

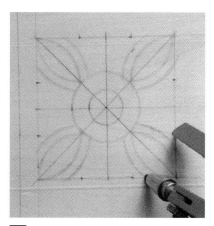

10 Place a compass on the same dots and draw the curved lines one more time.

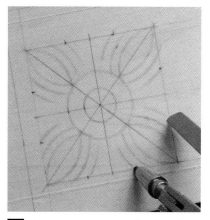

11 Place a compass on the dots for the third time and draw the curved lines and sides of the triangles.

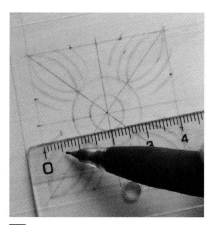

12 Measure 5mm inside from the side of the square to find the apex of the triangles.

13 Draw short lines using a compass to mark apexes on each of the triangles.

14 Connect the apexes of the triangles with their bases/dots, where the perpendicular lines cross the sides of the square.

The pattern in the corners and around the circle is ready. Now draw the central pattern. Divide the space that was formed between the outer and inner circles in half, mark a dot **15** and draw another circle. Then divide each of the eight sections in half by marking dots on the outer and inner circles **16**. Connect the resulting dots with those that go in the middle circle **17**. This will result in small rhombuses **18**.

Decorate these rhombuses with additional triangles or two-sided chips. Mark two dots 1–1.5mm one after the other on the outer sides of the rhombus by eye, starting from the corner of the rhombus in the middle circle **19**.

The pattern is now ready for carving **20**.

NOTE
In this pattern you do not need to prepare lines for stop cuts because, where there are rhombuses, there are small straight-wall chips, and stop cuts are not needed there. Where there are triangles, there are also straight-wall chips; and where there are sharp ovals, the diagonal lines pass through them and divide them in half exactly at the place where there are stop cuts.

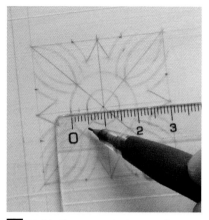

15 Divide the space between the first and second circles in half, then draw another circle using a compass.

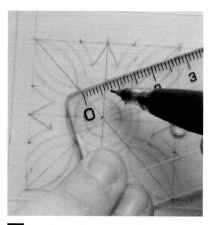

16 Divide each section of the central circle in half.

17 Connect the dots on the first and third circles with the dots on the second circle to draw the rhombuses.

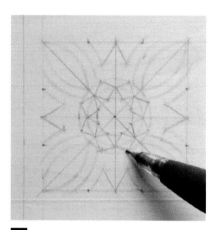

18 The completely drawn rhombuses.

19 Draw lines inside each rhombus for line carving.

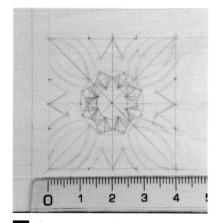

20 The pattern is drawn.

CARVING PROCESS

First, make stop cuts. In this pattern, they need to be made only inside two-sided chips, as mentioned in the drawing process. Stop cuts are made with a slight pressure of the knife where the tops of the ovals are, and the deepest point is in the middle of the diagonal/central line of the oval **21**. All stop cuts inside these ovals/two-sided chips are made perpendicular to the surface of the wood. Start undercutting one of the sides of any of the ovals at an angle of 60–65 degrees. You may notice later, while undercutting the second side, that it goes with the same movement of the knife – towards you or away from you, depending on which oval you started carving from **22**, **23**, **24**. When the first oval is done, carve the one diagonally opposite; again, the undercutting will go the same way as the first one. When you finish carving these, carve the other two: the undercutting direction will be different from the previous two. So as not to get lost in the movement of your knife, carve all the ovals in that order **25**.

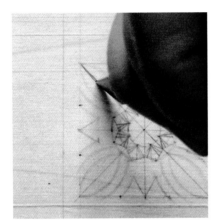

21 Make stop cuts inside each oval.

22 Start undercutting one of the sides of any of the ovals at an angle of 60–65 degrees.

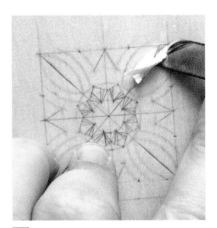

23 Undercut the second side at 60–65 degrees.

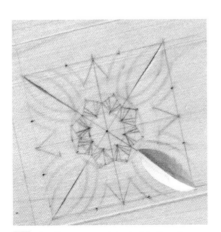

24 The first two-sided chip/oval is complete.

25 Now carve the rest of the ovals in sequence.

Next, carve the curved lines that go around the ovals. First, undercut the beginning and the end of the line very neatly at an angle of about 65 degrees, using only the tip of your knife **26**, **27**. Then carve the lines themselves, also at an angle of 60–65 degrees, leading the knife not on the line itself, but 1mm from it to the right, when the undercut goes towards you or away from you, and to the left of it, when the undercut also goes towards you or away from you – it depends on which contour line you are carving **28**, **29**. Carve the remaining lines **30**.

Now carve the triangles/straight-wall chips along the sides of the square on the inside, between the ovals. First, carve those where the bases of the triangles go along the grain. Hold the knife firmly at about 90 degrees to the surface of the board. Push the knife tip deep into the pattern **31**, then lower the heel of the blade along the pencil line to the base of the triangle. Next, carefully checking how smoothly the knife goes through the grain and setting the correct knife grip in your hand, push the knife towards the intersecting corner of the straight-wall sides to remove the chip **32**. Carve the remaining chips **33**.

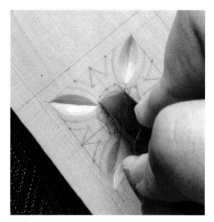

26 Undercut the end of the curved line around the oval.

27 Undercut the beginning very neatly at an angle of about 65 degrees, using only the tip of your knife.

28 Carve the lines themselves, also at an angle of 60–65 degrees. This is the first side.

29 This is the second side.

30 The completely carved lines around the ovals.

31 Hold the knife firmly at about 90 degrees to the surface of the board. Push the knife tip deep into the pattern.

32 Push the knife towards the intersecting corner of the straight-wall sides to remove the chip.

33 The completely carved straight-wall chips that go between the ovals.

Now proceed to the small straight-wall chips that go around the central circle. Again, repeating all the steps **34**, **35**, carve all the chips. Since they are very small here, carve them only with the tip of your knife so as not to break their sides **36**.

These resulting rhombuses have decorations in the form of two-sided chips/triangles. To carve them, divide the distance between the two lines by eye. Gently, using only the tip of the knife, make the cut, but do not work close to where the lines connect with each other **37**. Following the direction of the grain, make undercuts on both sides from the cut at an angle of 60–65 degrees.

The carving is now complete **38**.

34 Start carving the straight-wall chips in the central pattern between the rhombuses; first, for example, the top ones.

35 Then carve the bottom chips.

36 The completely carved straight-wall chips in the central pattern.

37 Make stop cuts between the lines inside the rhombuses, then make undercuts on both sides from the stop cuts at 60–65 degrees.

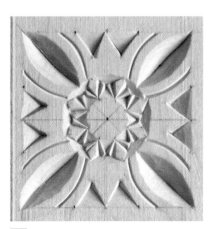

38 The carving is now complete.

SHARP CORNERS

This simple pattern consists of a continuous thin two-sided chip and an inner circle with eight three-sided chips. Here you will learn how to avoid chipping in the corners while carving.

TOOLS AND MATERIALS

- BASSWOOD BOARD (AT LEAST 100–120MM SQUARE AND 15MM THICK)

- 0.5MM MECHANICAL PENCIL WITH H OR HB LEAD

- RULER

- COMPASS

- SKEW KNIFE

- SANDPAPER OR LEATHER STRIPS FOR SHARPENING

DRAWING PROCESS

If you would prefer to transfer this pattern to the basswood board, the template is on page 169, and guidelines on page 12. Otherwise, if you prefer to draw the pattern directly on to the basswood board, follow the instructions below.

First draw a square with the sides 4cm long. Then draw two perpendicular lines that intersect at the centre and two diagonal lines that connect the opposite corners of the square **1**.

Next, prepare a circle for the central pattern, which features eight three-corners chips. Mark a dot 7.5mm either side of the centre of the square **2**, then draw a circle using a compass **3**. Next, mark a dot 5mm from the centre **4** and draw another circle inside the one already drawn **5**. We will immediately prepare this central pattern for carving and draw lines for stop cuts, since there are no other elements with stop cuts. Divide each section in half, put dots on the inner circle **6** and connect

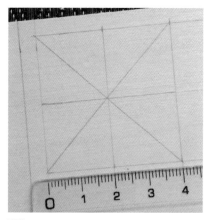

1 Draw a square with sides that are 4cm-long, then draw two perpendicular and two diagonal lines.

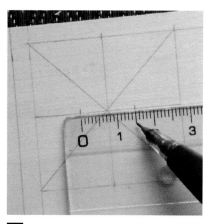

2 Mark dots 7.5mm to the left and right of the vertical perpendicular line.

3 Using a compass, draw a circle with a 7.5mm radius.

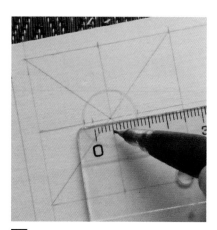

4 Mark a dot 5mm from the centre of the pattern.

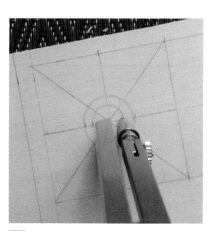

5 Then draw another circle using a compass.

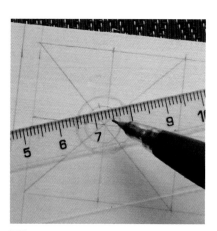

6 Divide the section inside the central circle in half and mark dots on the second circle.

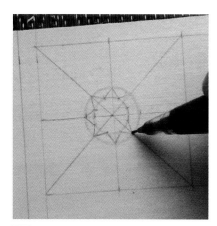

7 Connect the dots on the inner circle with those on the outer circle.

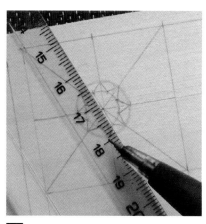

8 Draw the line for stop cuts inside each triangle.

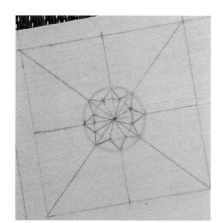

9 The finished drawn central circle with eight three-corner chips.

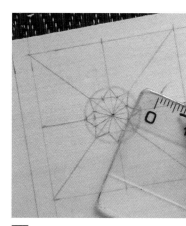

10 Mark a dot 7mm from the dot where the perpendicular lines divide the sides of the main square in half.

them to the bases of the triangles on the outer circle **7**. Connect the dots on the inner circle of each section with the opposite ones **8**. By doing this we will obtain the perpendicular lines of each triangle of this pattern for stop cuts **9**.

Now draw the triangles for the straight-wall chips, which form the pattern around the central circle. First, mark a dot 7mm from the dot where the perpendicular lines divide the sides of the main square in half, to the left and right sides of the perpendicular line **10**.

Or, to save time, mark a dot only on one side, and then make the rest of the marks with a compass **11**. Now, to find the tip of the triangle, you need to draw another dot: mark this dot 15.5–16mm from the centre to the previously prepared dots **12**.

Again, to save time, use a compass to draw the lines that will cross them **13**.

Begin to connect the resulting dots, first with the dots where the perpendicular lines divide the sides of the main square in half **14**, and then with the corners of the square **15**.

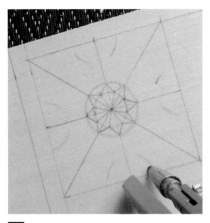

11 To save time, mark a dot only on one side, then make the other dots with a compass.

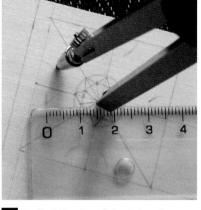

12 To find the tip of the triangle, draw another dot: mark this dot 1.55–1.6cm from the centre to the previously prepared dots.

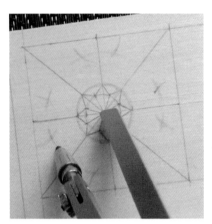

13 Again, to save time, use a compass to draw lines that will cross them.

14 Connect the resulting dots with the dots where the perpendicular lines divide the sides of the main square in half.

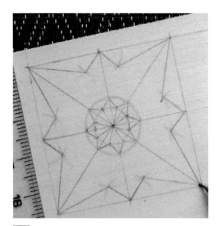

15 Connect them with the corners of the square.

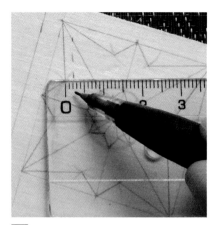

16 Mark short lines 2–2.5mm from each side.

Now we need to draw more lines on the inside of the resulting shape that will repeat this shape. Mark short lines 2–2.5mm from each side **16**, then connect them **17**.

The pattern is now ready for carving **18**.

17 Connect the lines.

18 The pattern is drawn.

CARVING PROCESS

To begin, make stop cuts in the central pattern – the circle with eight three-corner chips. The rest of the elements in this pattern are straight-wall chips and line carving, so there is no need to do stop cuts for these.

Begin to undercut and then carve the straight-wall chips that go along the sides of the main square on the inside. Since the sides of these straight-wall chips are long, push the knife tip deep into the wood **19**, then gently lead the tip of the blade along the line of the straight-wall chip until you reach its base, keeping at almost 90 degrees **20**.

The first straight-wall chips to carve are those where the bases go along the grain. I started to carve the upper straight-wall chip; when I reached the middle of the base, I felt that my knife was slowly breaking the grain **21** so I had to change my knife grip and its movement towards me (the wrong cut was away from me) **22**. On the opposite straight-wall chips, following my general rule, the movement of the knife was already away from me, and it went smoothly along the grain without breaking it **23**. Next, carve the remaining four straight-wall chips **24**.

19 Hold the knife firmly at about 90 degrees to the surface of the wood. Push the knife tip deep into the wood.

20 Gently lead the tip of the blade along the line of a straight-wall chip until you reach its base, keeping at an angle of almost 90 degrees.

21 You may feel that your knife is slowly breaking the grain.

22 If so, change the knife grip to complete carving the chip.

23 Carve the bottom chip.

24 Carve the remaining straight-wall chips.

25 Carve the circle with eight three-sided chips, starting with one of the chips whose base goes against the grain.

26 The completely carved circle with eight three-sided chips.

Now carve the central circle with the eight three-corner chips. Remember the rules of carving a pattern like this (see page 23), and start carving with one of the chips whose base goes against the grain **25**; it will be easier later to control carving the next chips when the sides go along the grain **26**.

Next, start on the line carving. First, for example, undercut the first line 1mm from it on the right **27**. Then make an undercut on the second line, next to the first one, which overlaps it, by slightly grabbing the first line with the tip of the knife to avoid chipping. When the undercutting on the right of all the lines is complete, start undercutting on the left to completely carve out the contour lines **28**.

The carving is now complete **29**.

27 Undercut the first line 1mm from it on the right.

28 When undercutting on the right of all the lines has been done, start undercutting on the left to completely carve out the contours.

29 The carving is now complete.

HEAD OF A FLOWER

This pattern consolidates the knowledge gained by carving the previous patterns: a continuous thin two-sided chip, triangles that are connected by bases and rhombuses with chips inside them.

TOOLS AND MATERIALS

- BASSWOOD BOARD (AT LEAST 100–120MM SQUARE AND 15MM THICK)

- 0.5MM MECHANICAL PENCIL WITH H OR HB LEAD

- RULER

- COMPASS

- SKEW KNIFE

- SANDPAPER OR LEATHER STRIPS FOR SHARPENING

DRAWING PROCESS

If you would prefer to transfer this pattern to the basswood board, the template is on page 169, and guidelines on page 12. Otherwise, if you prefer to draw the pattern directly on to the basswood board, follow the instructions below.

First draw a square with sides that are 4cm long. Then draw two perpendicular lines that intersect at the centre and two diagonal lines that connect the opposite corners of the square **1**. Using a compass, draw a 2cm-radius circle inside the square **2**. Next, without changing the radius on the compass, place it on one of the corners of the square and draw a curved line in one of the quarters of the circle **3**. Repeat these steps in the other three quarters of the circle **4**.

Now prepare curved lines, which will be for contour carving: mark a dot 2.2cm from the corner of the square on the diagonal line (or 6mm from the centre of the main square) **5**. Using a compass, draw curved lines in each quarter of the circle from the corners of the square inside the inner rhombus (formed by the previously made sharp ovals) **6**.

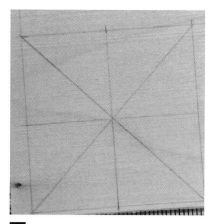

1 Draw a square with sides that are 4cm long, then draw two perpendicular and two diagonal lines.

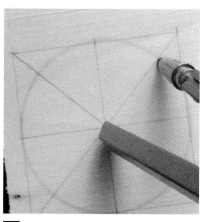

2 Using a compass, draw a 2cm-radius circle inside the square.

3 Place the compass on the corner of the square and, using a radius of 2cm, draw a curved line inside the circle.

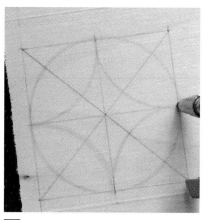

4 Mark the three other lines.

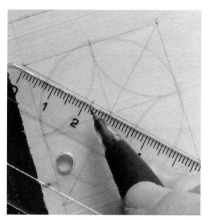

5 Mark a dot 2.2cm from the corner of the square on the diagonal line.

6 Draw curved lines in each quarter of the circle from the corners of the square inside the inner rhombus.

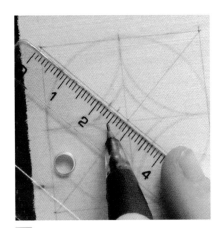

7 Mark one more dot 2.5cm from the corner of the square on the diagonal line.

8 Draw four more curved lines in each quarter of the circle from the corners of the square inside the inner rhombus.

To draw a rhombus in the centre of the pattern, where the two triangles are connected by their bases, make a mark 2.5cm from the corner of the square on the diagonal line (or 3.5cm from the centre) **7**. Draw curved lines from the corners of the square using a compass **8**.

Now draw the squares/rhombuses inside the sharp ovals. First, connect the tops of the ovals together **9**. Then, using a ruler, begin to connect with broken lines (which will end where the diagonal line inside the ovals pass) those dots where the circle intersects the diagonal lines of the main square. First draw the outer sides of the rhombuses **10**, then the inner ones **11**.

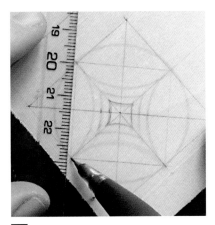

9 Connect the tops of the ovals together with a line.

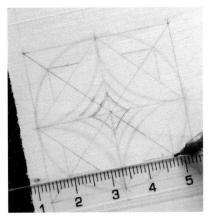

10 Draw the outer sides of the rhombuses.

11 Then draw the inner sides.

To finish drawing these squares/rhombuses, add decorations in the form of triangles/two-sided chips: mark two dots one after the other on the outer sides of the rhombus, starting from the corners on the diagonal lines of the ovals **12**. Connect them to the dot where the diagonal line of the main square passes and crosses the outer line of the oval **13**.

Now add lines for stop cuts inside the small rhombus in the centre of the entire pattern. Mark dots 2mm to the right and left sides of the vertical perpendicular line of the main square, and connect these to the common base of the triangles.

The pattern is now ready for carving **14**.

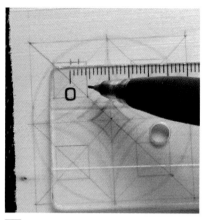

12 Mark two dots one after the other on the outer sides of the rhombus.

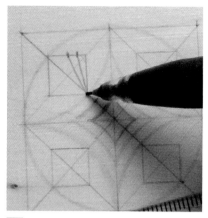

13 Connect them to the dot where the diagonal line of the main square passes and crosses the outer line of the oval.

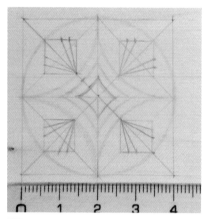

14 The pattern is drawn.

CARVING PROCESS

First, make stop cuts in the sharp ovals. Start making them from the tops of the rhombuses, from the deepest part of the incomplete triangles (the triangles without bases) to the tops of ovals by placing your knife perpendicular to the surface of wood . Then make stop cuts on the sides of the rhombuses. Do not do this perpendicular to the surface of the board, but at an angle of approximately 90 degrees 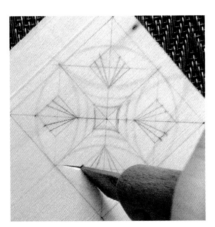, .

Start carving the sides of these triangles without bases at an angle of 60–65 degrees, following the direction of the grain and changing the knife grip where necessary. For example, the sides of two triangles that go on one side of the oval can be undercut immediately, because the knife grip does not change in your hand . Then rotate the board and undercut the other two sides of the triangles on the second side of the oval . If the chips did not pop out, repeat the undercuts or the stop cuts at the meeting points 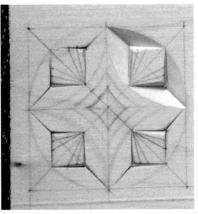.

15 First, make stop cuts in the sharp ovals.

16 Make stop cuts on the sides of the rhombuses at an angle of approximately 90 degrees.

17 This shows the stop cuts inside the sharp ovals.

18 Undercut the sides of the two triangles, which go on one side of the oval.

19 Rotate the board and then undercut the other two sides of the triangles, which go on the second side of the oval.

20 The first two triangles, without bases, inside the oval are carved.

Carve the remaining triangles inside the other ovals **21**. On the resulting rhombuses there are decorations in the form of two-sided chips/triangles. Divide the distance between the two lines by eye and gently, using only the tip of the knife, make the cut, but do not get too close to where they connect with each other **22**. Following the direction of the grain, make undercuts on both sides from the cut at an angle of 60–65 degrees **23**, **24**. Repeat these steps on the remaining rhombuses **25**.

Now carve the central rhombus, where two triangles are connected by bases. Prepare stop cuts. Start undercutting one of the triangles from the base, holding the knife at a 45-degree angle **26**, then carve its sides **27**. Following the same steps, carve the second triangle **28**.

21 Carve the remaining triangles inside the other ovals.

22 Using the tip of the knife, cut between the lines inside the rhombus.

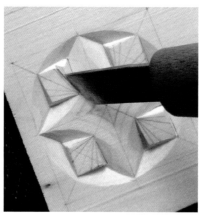

23 Make undercuts on both sides from the cut at 60–65 degrees.

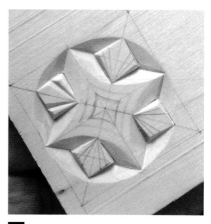

24 The first oval with the rhombus is complete.

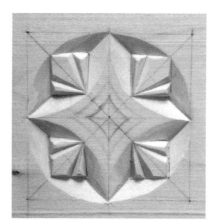

25 Repeat the steps to carve the remaining rhombuses.

26 Start undercutting one of the triangles from the base, holding the knife at 45 degrees.

27 Then carve its sides.

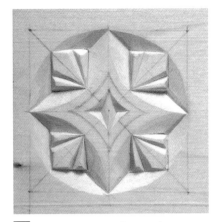

28 Carve the second triangle in the same way.

Now work on the contour lines. First undercut the first line 1mm from it on the right **29**. Then make the cut on the second line, next to the first one, which overlaps it, by slightly grabbing the first line with the tip of the knife to avoid chipping **30**. When the undercutting on the right of all the lines is complete, starts cutting on the left to completely carve out the contour lines **31**.

The carving is now complete **32**.

29 Undercut the first line 1mm from it on the right.

30 Make the cut on the second line next to the first one, slightly grabbing the first line with the tip of the knife.

31 Start cutting on the left to completely carve out the contour lines.

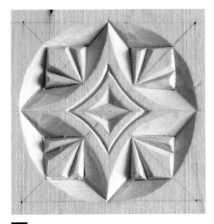

32 The carving is now complete.

ASYMMETRY

This pattern opens a series of designs more complex than the previous ones. In this, and all the remaining patterns in the book, it is necessary to carve the chips sequentially because, for the most part, they are connected to each other.

TOOLS AND MATERIALS

- BASSWOOD BOARD (AT LEAST 100–120MM SQUARE AND 15MM THICK)

- 0.5MM MECHANICAL PENCIL WITH H OR HB LEAD

- RULER

- COMPASS

- SKEW KNIFE

- SANDPAPER OR LEATHER STRIPS FOR SHARPENING

DRAWING PROCESS

If you would prefer to transfer this pattern to the basswood board, the template is on page 169, and guidelines on page 12. Otherwise, if you prefer to draw the pattern directly on to the basswood board, follow the instructions below.

First draw a square with the sides 6cm long. Then draw two perpendicular lines that intersect at the centre and two diagonal lines that connect the opposite corners of the square 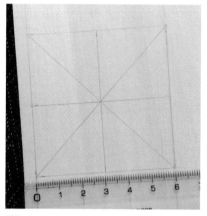.

Next, prepare a circle for the central and main pattern. Using a compass, draw a circle with a 3cm radius inside the square. Next, fill the sections of the circle with patterns. First, draw four-sided chips of different thicknesses along the inner perimeter of the circle. Mark a dot 2.2cm from the centre **2**. Using a compass, draw the curved lines of this radius in every other section, starting with the one to the left of the vertical perpendicular line **3**. In the remaining sections, mark a dot 2.6cm from the centre of the pattern **4** and draw curved lines using a compass **5**, **6**.

1 Draw a square with sides that are 6cm long, then draw two perpendicular and two diagonal lines.

2 Draw a circle with a 3cm radius inside a square, then mark a dot 2.2cm from the centre.

3 Draw curved lines of this radius in every other section.

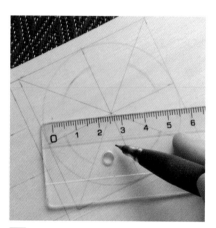

4 Mark a dot 2.6cm from the centre of the pattern in the remaining sections.

5 Draw four more curved lines.

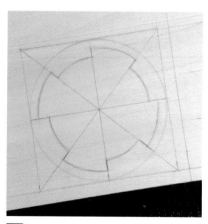

6 The main shape of the pattern.

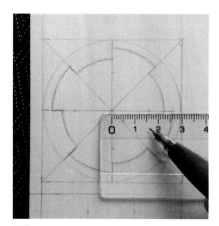

7 Mark the first dot for the shorter oval 1.6cm from the centre on the vertical and horizontal perpendicular lines.

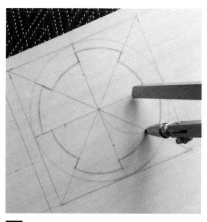

8 Place the compass on a dot and draw curved lines clockwise from the compass's position.

Next, draw the central sharp semi-ovals of different lengths. Mark the first dot for the shorter oval 1.6cm from the centre on the vertical and horizontal perpendicular lines **7**. Put the compass on a dot and draw a curved line starting from the centre of the pattern (clockwise from where the compass is placed) to the point where the diagonal line of the main pattern goes **8**. Repeat these steps on the remaining three dots **9**.

9 Repeat this in the other three sections.

10 Mark a dot 1.9cm from the centre on the horizontal and vertical perpendicular lines.

Now mark a dot 1.9cm from the centre also on the horizontal and vertical perpendicular lines **10**. Placing the compass on a dot, draw a curved line to the right (anticlockwise from where the compass is placed) to the point where the diagonal line of the main pattern goes **11**.

Now draw lines for line carving that will repeat the contour of the wide and the narrow four-sided chips. Mark a dot 3mm from each side, and draw curved lines with a compass **12**.

11 Place the compass on a dot, and draw curved lines anticlockwise from where the compass is placed.

12 Draw the lines for line carving, repeating the contour of the thin four-sided chips.

Where there are wide four-sided chips, draw a line a little beyond the perpendicular lines **13**, **14**. Take a ruler and, on the line that goes a bit beyond the perpendicular lines, mark a dot 3mm from the perpendicular line **15**. Having drawn a parallel line, connect the top and bottom curved lines together **16**, **17**.

13 Mark a dot 3mm from the side of the wider chip.

14 Draw the lines for line carving, repeating the contour of the wide four-sided chips.

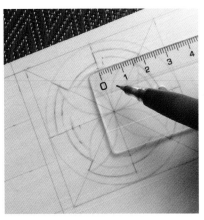

15 Mark a dot 3mm to the right from the perpendicular line to connect the top and bottom lines.

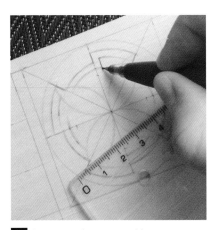

16 Connect the top and bottom lines.

17 The lines for line carving are completely prepared.

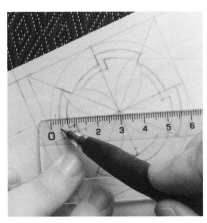

18 Divide the thin chips to find the lines for stop cuts.

19 Draw the lines for stop cuts inside each thin four-sided chip.

20 Divide the wider chips to find the lines for stop cuts.

Start drawing lines inside the chips for additional stop cuts. Start with the thin four-sided chips: divide them in half **18** and draw lines using a compass **19**. Repeat these steps inside the wide four-sided chips **20**. The central lines for additional stop cuts are ready; now mark where the deepest spots are inside the four-sided chips.

Start again with the thin four-sided chips: mark a dot 3mm from the horizontal perpendicular and the diagonal lines of the main pattern inside each thin chip **21**, then connect these dots with the bases/short sides **22**. Repeat these steps inside the wide four-sided chips, but mark dots 4mm from the diagonal and perpendicular lines **23**, **24**, **25**.

21 Mark dots 3mm from the perpendicular and diagonal lines to find the lines for stop cuts for the bases of the thin chips.

22 Connect the dots with the bases of the thin chips.

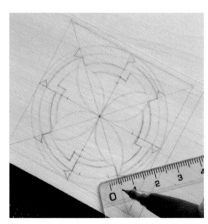

23 Mark dots 4mm from the perpendicular and diagonal lines to find the lines for stop cuts for the bases of the wide chips.

24 Connect the dots with the bases of the wide chips.

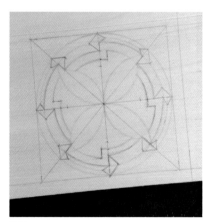

25 The completely prepared thin and wide chips for carving.

Draw lines inside the semi-ovals for additional stop cuts: divide in half the widest place of one of the semi-ovals **26**, and draw a line by hand that follows the shape of the semi-oval's curved side **27**. Repeat these steps on the remaining semi-ovals.

The pattern is now ready for carving **28**.

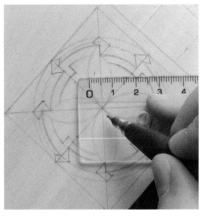

26 Divide in half the widest place of one of the semi-ovals.

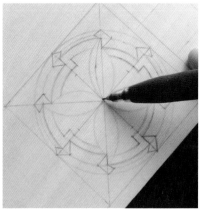

27 Draw the line for stop cuts inside the semi-oval.

28 The pattern is drawn.

WEAK AND STRONG CONNECTIONS

For the most part, the weak connection in the patterns is at the ends of the lines, where the chips are connected to each other, while edges of the carving are chipped less often. It does not matter whether they are connected to each other by the bases or by the sides. We need to make sure that this is no longer a weak connection but is transformed into a strong connection. In order to do this, you need to carve the place where they connect without chipping. To do this when undercutting, it is necessary to hold the knife at the right angle, for it to be sharp and for the wood you are carving to have been dried properly. In this pattern, we have a slight advantage: the place where the thin and wide chips are connected together, in a sense, is no longer a weak connection, because the ends of the short sides of the thin chips do not connect to the ends of the short sides of the wide chips (they are not the same length); therefore it is possible to avoid chipping just with sequential undercutting.

CARVING PROCESS

Make stop cuts inside all the chips of the pattern. Inside each of the semi-ovals, make stop cuts with a slight pressure of the knife where the tops of the semi-ovals go; the deepest place is the middle of the diagonal/central line of the semi-oval **29**. All stop cuts inside these are made perpendicular to the surface of the board.

Start carving the pattern from one of the thin four-sided chips; namely, undercutting its short sides **30**. Then undercut its long sides **31**. All undercuts inside these thin and the other wide four-sided chips are made at an angle of 60–65 degrees, following the grain direction. When one thin four-sided chip is carved **32**, carve the remaining thin chips. Notice where the

short sides of the chips go along the grain: first carefully check when the knife goes easily through the grain – whether away from you or towards you – and only then make an undercut **33**. Carve out the remaining thin chips **34**.

29 Make stop cuts inside all the chips of the pattern before carving.

30 Undercut the short side of the thin chip.

31 Then undercut its long side at an angle of 60–65 degrees.

32 The first chip is complete.

33 Start undercutting the other thin chips following the direction of the grain.

34 The four thin four-sided chips are carved.

Next, start carving the wide chips. I left these to be carved last in this sequence, because I follow this principle in my carving system: when smaller chips are combined in patterns with larger chips, the smaller ones are carved first, then the larger ones – there is an effect in the pattern that the larger ones cover the small chips.

To carve the wide chips, start undercutting them from the short sides **35**. Carve the first chip **36** and then the remaining wide ones, following the grain direction **37**.

Next carve the two-sided chips; that is, the semi-ovals. Start carving them from one of the shorter chips, keeping the knife at a 65-degree angle to the surface of the wood. Start from the side where one semi-oval connects with the other, longer semi-oval **38**, then undercut it from the other side **39**. Then turn the board to make it comfortable to undercut a longer chip. Start carving it from the common side **40**, then carve its second side **41**.

Following the steps for undercutting chips of different sizes, carve out the remaining semi-ovals **42**.

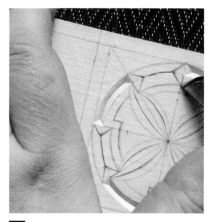

35 Start undercutting the short side of a wide chip.

36 Carve the first chip.

37 Carve the remaining wide chips, following the grain direction.

38 Start carving the semi-ovals from one of the shorter chips, keeping the knife at a 65-degree angle to the surface of the wood.

39 Then undercut the shorter semi-oval from the other side.

40 Start carving the longer semi-oval from the side common with the previously carved short semi-oval.

41 Carve the second side of the longer chip.

42 Carve out the remaining semi-ovals.

Now carve the lines that repeat the shape of the pattern formed by the thin and wide four-sided chips. First, for example, undercut the long first line 1mm to the right **43**. Then make an undercut on the second short line, next to the first one, which overlaps it, by slightly grabbing the first line with the tip of the knife to avoid chipping **44**.

When the undercutting on the right of all the lines is complete, rotate the board and start undercutting on the left to completely carve out the lines **45**, **46**.

The carving is now complete **47**.

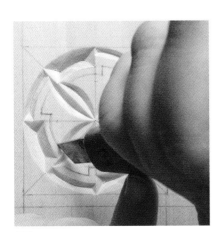

43 Undercut the long first line 1mm to the right of the line.

44 Then make the undercut on the second short line, next to the first one.

45 Rotate the board and start undercutting on the left to completely carve out the lines.

46 The first line with sharp corners is carved out.

47 The carving is now complete.

FLOWER

At first glance, this pattern does not seem very complex. In fact it is, but the difficulty lies in the sequence of carving the triangles and in the sizes of the triangles themselves – they are long and relatively large.

TOOLS AND MATERIALS

- BASSWOOD BOARD (AT LEAST 100–120MM SQUARE AND 15MM THICK)

- 0.5MM MECHANICAL PENCIL WITH H OR HB LEAD

- RULER

- COMPASS

- SKEW KNIFE

- SANDPAPER OR LEATHER STRIPS FOR SHARPENING

DRAWING PROCESS

If you would prefer to transfer this pattern to the basswood board, the template is on page 169, and guidelines on page 12. Otherwise, if you prefer to draw the pattern directly on to the basswood board, follow the instructions below.

First draw a square with sides that are 6cm long. Then draw two perpendicular lines that intersect at the centre and two diagonal lines that connect the opposite corners of the square. Mark a dot 2cm from the top right corner of the square **1**, then another dot 2.1cm from the point where the vertical perpendicular line divides the top side of the square in half **2**. Repeat these steps, but mark the first dot 2cm from the top left corner. Measure a radius of 4.8cm and, using a compass, draw curved lines from the resulting points to the opposite quarter **3**.

Mark a dot 2.25cm from the top right corner, making it closer to the right side of the square **4**. Repeat this in the left quarter. Measure a radius of 3.15cm and, using a compass, draw two short lines from the point where the vertical perpendicular line divides the top line of the square in half, crossing the previously prepared ones **5**. Measure a radius of 4.5cm and, by placing the compass on one and then on another prepared dot, draw curved lines on the opposite sides **6**.

1 Mark the first dot 2cm from the top right corner of the square.

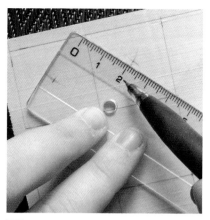
2 Mark the second dot 2.1cm from the point where the vertical perpendicular line divides the top side of the square in half.

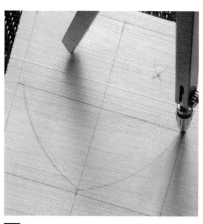
3 Place the compass on the dot, and draw curved lines from the resulting points to the opposite quarter.

4 Mark a dot 2.25cm from the top right corner closer to the right side of the square.

5 Draw two short lines crossing the previously prepared ones.

6 Place a compass on one and then on another prepared dot, and draw curved lines on the opposite sides.

7 Mark the last dots on the horizontal perpendicular line 3mm from the right and left sides of the square.

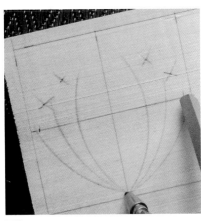

8 Draw curved lines on one and then the other side of the dots with a compass.

For the next dots, for the last two curved lines, mark on the horizontal perpendicular line 3mm from the right and left sides of the square **7**. Measure a radius of 4.1cm, and draw curved lines on each side of the dots with a compass **8**.

To draw the top of the pattern, mark a dot 6mm from the point on the top side of the square, where the vertical perpendicular line divides the top side of the square in half **9**. Next, mark a dot 6–7mm on the horizontal perpendicular line from the last/inner line **10**. Repeating the contour of this line, draw a curved line by hand, starting from the top of the pattern and ending at the base. On the other side, the line mirrors the one on the left: starting from the central perpendicular line, make short dashed lines from top to bottom measuring the width of the semi-oval on the left **11**. Connect all the resulting dots together into a single line **12**.

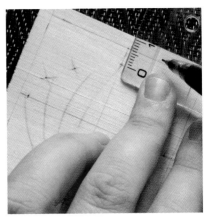

9 Mark a dot 6mm from the top side of the square and draw the top of the pattern.

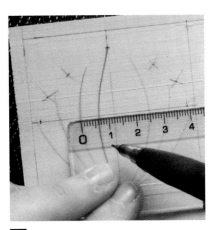

10 Mark a dot 6–7mm on the horizontal perpendicular line from the inner line.

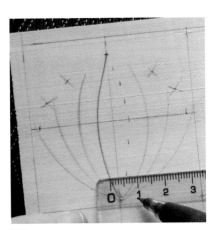

11 Measure the width of the semi-oval on the left, and draw short lines on the right.

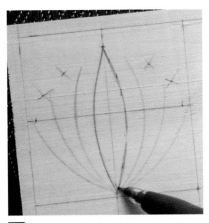

12 Connect the short lines together.

Now draw the bases of the long triangles. Measure a radius of 4.1cm for the first outer triangles. Starting from the base of the pattern, draw short curved lines, using a compass, on one triangle and on the other side **13**. For the second triangle, measure a radius of 4.4cm and, starting from the base of the pattern, draw short curved lines with a compass on the second triangle and the other side **14**. For the third and last triangle, measure a radius of 4.75cm and, starting from the base of the pattern, draw short curved lines on one triangle and on the triangle on the other side **15**.

Next, draw a triangle at the bottom of the pattern; this one has no base. Mark a dot on the central perpendicular line 1.1cm from the base of the pattern **16**, then mark two dots on the right and left sides of the central sharp oval, 1.6cm from the base of the pattern **17**. Connect the resulting dots together **18**.

13 Measure a 4.1cm radius for the first outer triangles, drawing short lines to mark the bases of the triangles.

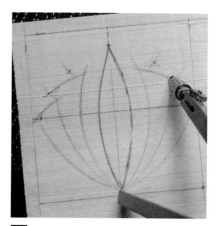

14 Measure a radius of 4.4cm for the second triangles from the left and right of the perpendicular line.

15 Draw short lines to mark the bases of the triangles.

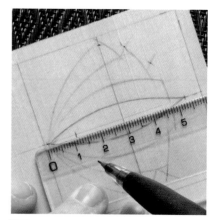

16 Mark a dot on the central perpendicular line 1.1cm from the base of the pattern.

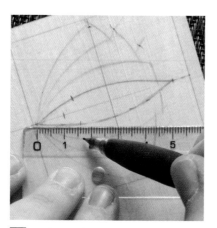

17 Mark two dots on the right and left sides of the central sharp oval, 1.6cm from the base of the pattern.

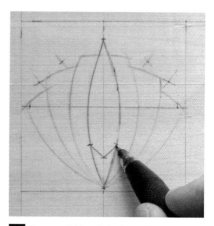

18 Connect the dots together.

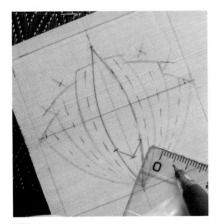

19 Divide the space inside each triangle in half.

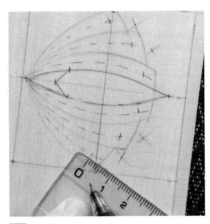

20 Mark the dots 4mm from each triangle's base.

Now, draw the lines for additional stop cuts inside the long triangles. Divide each triangle in half **19**, then from the top, where the bases of the triangles are, mark the dots 4mm from each base **20**. Connect these dots with the bases, then, inside all the triangles, connect the short lines together **21**.

Return to the central oval and decorate it with additional curved lines. By eye, starting from the deepest point of the bottom triangle, mark short lines 4–5mm from each other on the right and left sides of the oval. Connect them by hand with a dot marked on the central perpendicular line (the deepest point of the triangle) **22**, **23**.

The pattern is ready for carving.

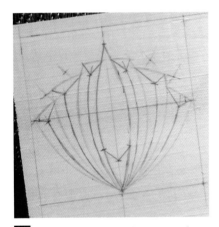

21 Connect the short lines together.

22 Mark short lines 4–5mm from each other on the right and left sides of the oval.

23 All the short lines marked on the pattern.

CARVING PROCESS

First, make stop cuts inside all the triangles of the pattern. Since the triangles are long, you will not be able to do this simply by pushing the knife tip deep into the wood and lowering the heel. To make the stop cuts, place the knife tip in the deepest place and lower the heel. Do not remove the knife from the wood, but lead it, perpendicular to the surface of the wood, to the top of the triangle to avoid cutting the stop cuts right up to the place where the triangles are joined together. Also make stop cuts inside the triangle without a base, which is in the central oval at the very bottom **24**.

Undercut one of the outer triangles from the outside at a 45-degree angle, starting from the base of the triangle and gently moving to its top (where the triangles are connected together) **25**.

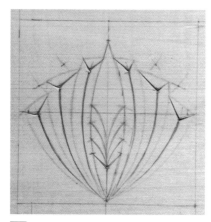

24 Make stop cuts inside all the triangles of the pattern.

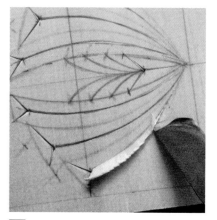

25 Undercut one of the outer triangles from the outside at an angle of 45 degrees.

26 The first triangle of the pattern is complete.

27 Finish undercutting the triangle from the inside, starting from the top of the triangle.

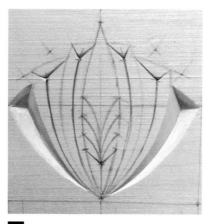

28 Two outer triangles are complete.

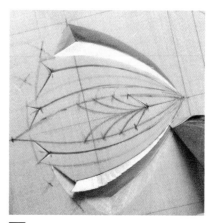

29 Start undercutting the next triangle, starting from the outer side.

30 Finish carving the second long side, starting from the top of the triangle.

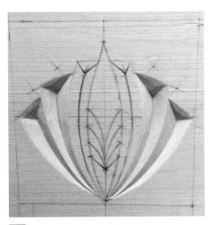

31 Carve the second opposite triangle.

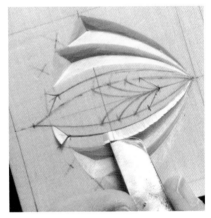

32 Place the knife at a 45-degree angle and start undercutting the facet of the third triangle from the steepest curve.

33 Finish undercutting the first side from the steepest curve.

34 Carve the second long side of the third triangle starting from the top.

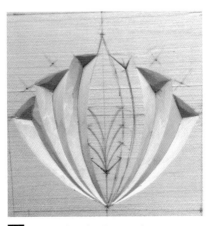

35 Carve the third triangle on the left.

Next, undercut the short side/base and then the second long side, starting from the top of the triangle, following the grain direction **26**. Repeat these steps on the opposite outer triangle. Finish undercutting it from the inside, starting from the top of the triangle, gently but surely leading your knife to the base of the triangle **27**, **28**.

Start undercutting the next triangle, beginning from the outer side (the one that connects to one of the sides of the previous triangle). Gently, with the knife tip, lead the knife to its top **29**, then undercut the base of the triangle and then the second long side, starting from the top **30**. Carve the second opposite triangle **31**.

The next triangle is even longer than the previous two, and in this case the side, which is partially common to the previous triangle, is slightly rounded. I suggest undercutting it this way: find the most curved place on the outside common side. Place the knife at an angle of 45 degrees, and start undercutting the facet from that position **32**. When the undercut is made, rotate the board, change the knife grip in your hand and finish undercutting the rest of the facet to the base of the triangle, also starting at the most curved place **33**. Finish cutting the triangle, first cutting the base and then the second long side, starting from the top **34**, **35**.

Then carve the opposite third triangle using the same steps **36**. Now carve the last triangle without the base at the very bottom of the design, also keeping the knife at a 45-degree angle **37**, **38**.

Next, start cutting the lines in the central oval, making cuts straight along the lines perpendicular to the surface of the wood **39**. Avoid cutting up to the point where the lines connect together **40**.

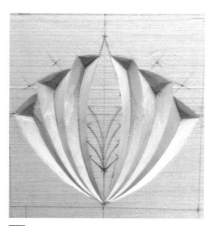

36 Then carve the opposite third triangle on the right.

37 Carve the last triangle without the base at the very bottom, keeping the knife at a 45-degree angle.

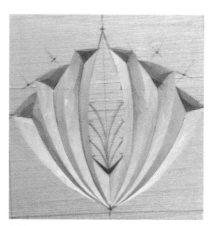

38 All the triangles are complete.

39 Make cuts straight along the lines perpendicular to the surface of the wood.

40 Avoid cutting up to the point where the lines connect together.

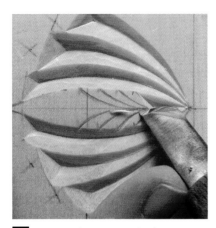

41 Start undercutting the lines about 1mm on the right and on the left from them.

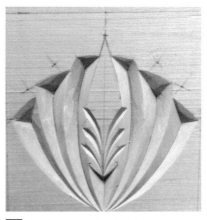

42 The lines inside the sharp oval are complete.

Then start undercutting the lines about 1mm on the right and on the left from them **41**, **42**. Now mark the top of the oval using undercuts at an angle of 65 degrees on each side of the lines **43**.

The carving is now complete **44**.

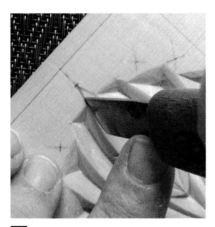

43 Carve the top of the oval using undercuts at an angle of 65 degrees.

44 The carving is now complete.

CARVING LARGE CHIPS

When it comes to carving these relatively large chips, the main thing (apart from the fact that the tool must be sharp) is to keep the knife at the correct angle and to confidently lead the knife to undercut a facet. If you undercut and lead your knife unconfidently, then the inner facet of the triangle (or the chip you are carving) will form wavy lines instead of being straight and smooth.

SQUARES

In this pattern there is no need to draw perpendicular and diagonal lines as in the previous designs, since they are not needed here. The main motif of the pattern is triangles that form squares, twisting anticlockwise.

TOOLS AND MATERIALS

- BASSWOOD BOARD (AT LEAST 100–120MM SQUARE AND 15MM THICK)

- 0.5MM MECHANICAL PENCIL WITH H OR HB LEAD

- RULER

- COMPASS

- SKEW KNIFE

- SANDPAPER OR LEATHER STRIPS FOR SHARPENING

DRAWING PROCESS

If you would prefer to transfer this pattern to the basswood board, the template is on page 169, and guidelines on page 12. Otherwise, if you prefer to draw the pattern directly on to the basswood board, follow the instructions below.

First, draw a square with 6cm sides **1**. Start marking the next dots: first, 1cm on the left side of the square from the top left corner down to the left side of the square; second, 1cm from the bottom left corner to the right side, on the bottom side of the square; third, 1cm from the bottom right corner up, on the right side of the square; fourth, 1cm from the top right corner to the left side, on the bottom side of the square **2**. All these steps – that is, the movement anticlockwise, only with different sizes – will need to be repeated several times.

Connect the resulting dots **3**. Next, on the resulting square, start to measure the following points: mark a dot 9mm from the top left corner down, on the left side of the previously drawn square **4**; then repeat all the steps with this size on the other sides **5**. Three squares are now ready (including the first) and you can begin the fourth. On the last square you drew, mark a dot

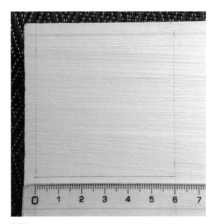

1 Draw a square with sides that are 6cm long.

2 Mark the first dots on the sides of the first square.

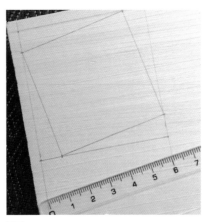

3 The second square, inside the first one, is drawn.

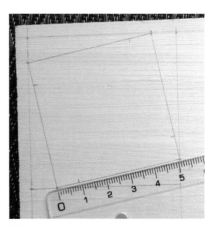

4 Start marking the next dot to draw the third square.

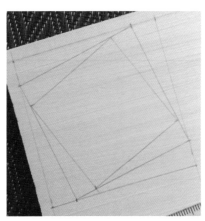

5 Connect the dots together, and the third square is ready.

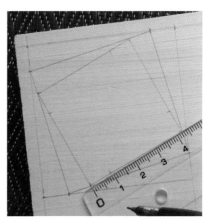

6 Mark out the dots for the fourth square.

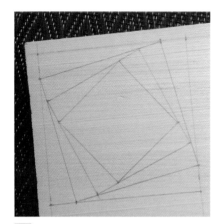

7 The fourth square is drawn.

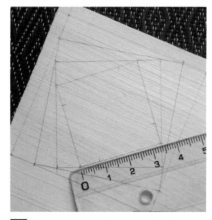

8 Mark the next dots on the fourth square to draw the fifth one.

9mm starting from the top left corner down to its left side. Repeat all the steps on the other sides of the square **6**, then connect the dots together **7**.

Now start the fifth square. On the square just drawn, mark all the dots 8mm anticlockwise from the corners **8**, then connect them together **9**. For the sixth square, mark all the dots 7mm anticlockwise from the corners of the square on the square just drawn **10** and connect them together.

For the seventh (last) square, mark all the dots 6mm anticlockwise from the corners on the previous square, then connect them together **11**. Draw two diagonal lines that connect the opposite corners in the resulting last square **12**.

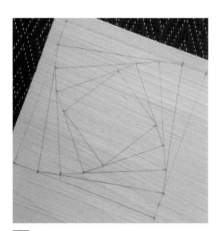

9 The fifth square is ready.

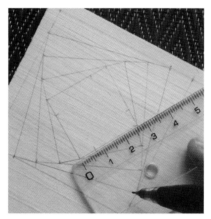

10 Mark the dots on the fifth square for drawing the sixth one.

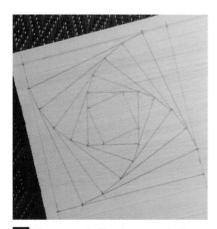

11 The seventh (last) square is done.

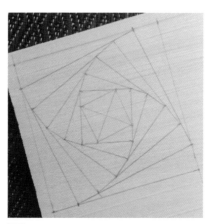

12 Connect the opposite corners of the seventh square together.

Now divide the sides of the last square in half, mark a dot, and then put dots 1.5mm to the right and left of it **13**. Connect these two points with the centre of the square **14**. Repeat these steps on the other sides of the square **15**.

Now start drawing lines inside the triangles for additional stop cuts. Start with the first (outermost) square and the first triangle to the left inside it. Divide the widest place of the triangle in half **16** and connect this dot to the top of the triangle. Next, mark a dot 5mm from the base **17**, then connect it with the base of the triangle. Repeat steps **16** and **17** for the remaining triangles in the section, which follow a kind of spiral to the centre. For the first three triangles in the section, mark dots 5mm from the base for the additional stop cuts. For the remaining three, mark dots 4mm from the base **18**. When the first section is done, repeat steps **16**, **17** and **18** for the other three sections of triangles **19**. The pattern is ready for carving.

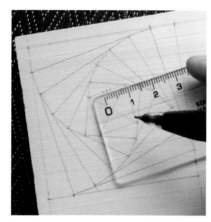

13 Divide the sides of the last square in half, marking a dot, and then put dots 1.5mm to the right and left of it.

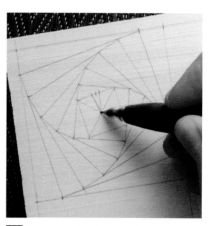

14 Connect the dots with the centre of the pattern.

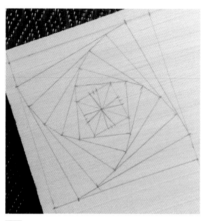

15 Repeat the steps on the other sides of the square.

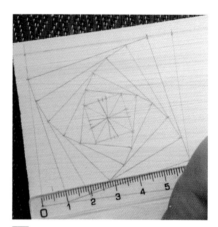

16 Divide the widest place of the triangle in half.

17 Mark a dot 5mm from the base of the triangle.

18 Divide and find the deepest places of the triangles in the first section and marking the dots.

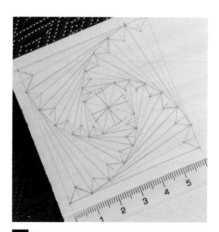

19 The pattern is drawn.

CARVING PROCESS

First, make stop cuts inside all the triangles. Place the knife tip in the deepest place and lower the heel **20**. Keep the knife perpendicular to the surface of the wood to the top of the triangle, but avoid cutting the stop cuts right up to it **21**. Make cuts in the remaining triangles **22**.

Start carving the pattern, for example, from the bottom triangle that goes along the grain at the bottom of the square. Undercut the side that goes straight along the grain at an angle of 45 degrees, carefully checking when the knife goes smoothly through the grain (in my case, the knife went smoothly when undercutting away from me) **23**.

Completely carve out the triangle, also at a 45-degree angle **24**. Then move to the left from this triangle, and undercut the base of the previous triangle; this will also go away from you (or towards you, depending on how you undercut the first chip) **25**.

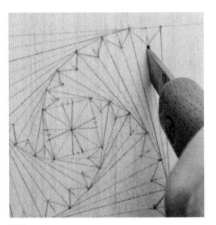

20 Place the knife tip in the deepest place of the first triangle and lower the heel.

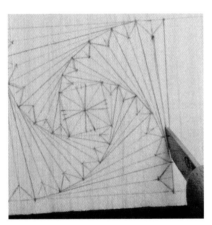

21 Keep the knife perpendicular to the surface of the wood to the top of the triangle, and avoid cutting the stop cut right up to it.

22 Now make stop cuts inside all of the triangles.

23 Undercut the side of the first triangle that goes straight along the grain at an angle of 45 degrees.

24 Carve the base and the second long side of the first triangle to completely carve it.

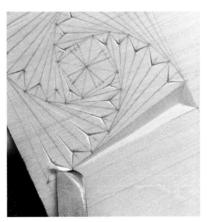

25 Move to the left from the carved triangle and undercut the base of the previous triangle.

Carve this triangle completely **26**.

Now move to the top horizontal line of the square and undercut the side of the triangle that goes along the grain. The knife grip in your hand on this side will already be different from how you held the knife on the bottom triangle when undercutting its side, which also goes along the grain **27**. Carve out this triangle, then move to the right and undercut the base of the chip, then the whole triangle **28**.

The most difficult triangles are now carved. The rest will require you to simply hold your knife correctly when undercutting. Follow the direction of the wood grain and have confidence when making cuts.

26 Carve it completely.

27 Move to the top horizontal line of the square first and undercut the side of the triangle that goes along the grain.

28 Move to the right from the previously carved triangle. First undercut the base of the chip, and only then the whole triangle.

29 Begin to carve the next triangles with their bases first.

30 Then carve the sides.

31 Moving anticlockwise, carve each triangle in turn until all the triangles are done.

Begin to carve the triangles in an anticlockwise direction. Begin with their bases **29**, then carve the side that is connected with the triangle on the outer square, and lastly carve the third long side **30**. Moving anticlockwise, carve each triangle in turn until all the triangles are complete **31**. Now cut out the very central pattern. Make perpendicular undercuts in the middle of each of the small triangles **32**, without bringing the tip of the knife right up to the point where these triangles are connected. Make cuts to the right and left of these stop cuts at an angle of 65 degrees **33**.

The carving is now complete **34**.

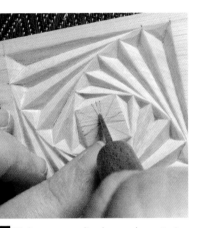

32 Make perpendicular undercuts in the middle of each small triangle in the central pattern.

33 Make the cuts to the right and left of the stop cuts, at an angle of 65 degrees.

34 The carving is now complete.

WIND

This pattern is more complex, since even on one triangle it is necessary to change the knife grip in your hand several times. The sides of the chips are very rounded, and almost all of them change their movement and go both along and against the grain.

TOOLS AND MATERIALS

- BASSWOOD BOARD (AT LEAST 100–120MM SQUARE AND 15MM THICK)

- 0.5MM MECHANICAL PENCIL WITH H OR HB LEAD

- RULER

- COMPASS

- SKEW KNIFE

- SANDPAPER OR LEATHER STRIPS FOR SHARPENING

DRAWING PROCESS

If you would prefer to transfer this pattern to the basswood board, the template is on page 169, and guidelines on page 12. Otherwise, if you prefer to draw the pattern directly on to the basswood board, follow the instructions below.

First draw a square with the sides 6cm long. Then draw two perpendicular lines that intersect at the centre and two diagonal lines that connect the opposite corners of the square. Next, prepare a circle for the central and main pattern. Using a compass, draw a circle with a 3cm radius inside the square **1**.

At the point where the circle crosses the diagonal line, mark a dot 1.8cm inside the circle (or 1.2cm from the centre of the pattern); this is the radius of the semicircles **2**. Draw semicircles in all the quarters of the circle using a compass; place it on the points where the circle crosses the diagonal lines **3**. Next, mark a dot 2mm from the resulting curved line **4**. Using a compass, again draw semicircles in all quarters of the circle **5**.

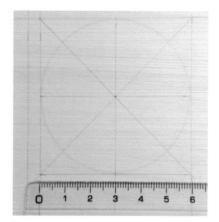

1 Draw a square with 6cm-long sides and then draw two perpendicular and horizontal lines. Draw a circle inside the square with a 3cm radius.

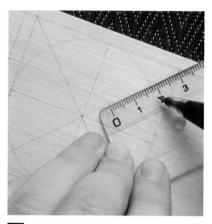

2 Mark a dot 1.8cm inside the circle on one of the diagonal lines.

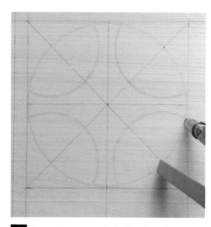

3 Now draw semicircles in all four quarters of the circle using a compass.

4 Mark a dot 2mm from the curved line of the semicircle.

5 Draw four more semicircles using a compass in all four quarters of the circle.

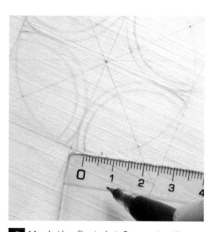

6 Mark the first dot 6mm starting from the right bottom of the outer semicircle, from its lowest point.

7 Mark the second dot 8.5mm from the lowest point of the outer semicircle.

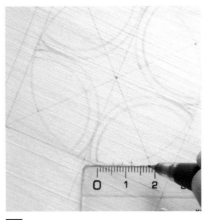

8 Mark the third dot 1.2cm from the lowest point of the outer semicircle.

Proceed to the drawing of the main pattern: the rounded triangles inside the resulting four semicircles. Start marking dots anticlockwise, starting from the right bottom of the outer semicircle, from its lowest point. Mark these dots one after another: the first dot 6mm **6**; the second 8.5mm **7**; the third 1.2cm **8**; the fourth 1.4cm **9**. Using a compass, draw semicircles using the radius of those marked dots **10**, **11**. Repeat these steps in the other three sections **12**.

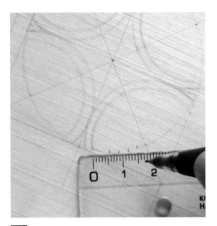

9 Mark the fourth dot 1.4cm from the lowest point of the outer semicircle.

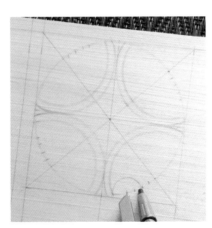

10 Using a compass, draw semicircles using the radius of the dots.

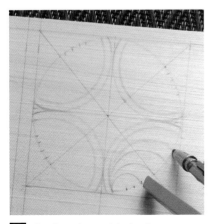

11 The fourth semicircle drawn.

12 Repeat all the steps in the remaining sections.

Now draw lines inside the chips for additional stop cuts. Divide the resulting triangles in half **13**, then mark dots 3mm from each base **14** and connect them with the bases of the triangles **15**, **16**.

Lastly, draw a square in the very centre of the pattern. To do this, connect the points where the inner semicircles intersect the diagonal lines **17**.

The pattern is now ready for carving **18**.

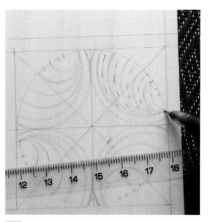

13 Divide each of the triangles in half.

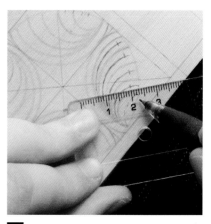

14 Mark dots 3mm from each triangle's base.

15 Connect the dots with the triangles' bases in the first semicircle.

16 Repeat this in the remaining semicircles.

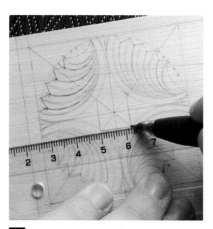

17 Draw a square in the very centre of the pattern.

18 The pattern is drawn.

19 Now make stop cuts inside all of the triangles.

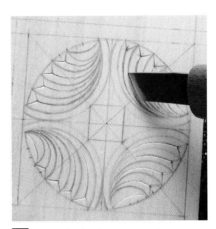

20 Place the knife at a 45-degree angle, and start undercutting the facet of the first triangle from the steepest curve.

21 Finish undercutting the rest of the first facet of the first triangle.

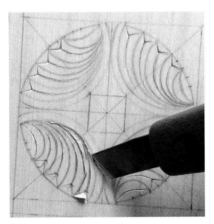

22 Rotate the board and undercut the second long side of the first triangle.

23 Change the knife grip and finish undercutting the side, starting from the base.

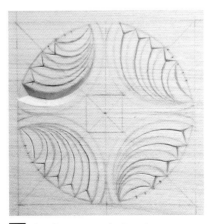

24 The first carved triangle.

CARVING PROCESS

Make stop cuts inside all the triangles **19**, but don't prepare inner triangles or make cuts for multi-level chips yet. Start carving this pattern from the section of triangles where the sides of the triangles, for the most part, go along the grain. They will prepare you for carving the triangles whose sides go against the grain.

Start to undercut from the longest triangle, from its inner side, which is connected to the following chip. Find the steepest curve and, placing the knife at 45 degrees, start undercutting the facet from this position **20**. When you undercut a triangle and reach the knife tip almost to where the triangles connect, change the angle of the knife to about 90 degrees to the surface of the wood so as not to go too much beyond the stop cut. When this first part of the undercut is done, change the knife grip in your hand and undercut the rest of the facet to the base of the triangle, also starting from the steepest curve **21**.

Next, carve the base of the triangle, then rotate the board and undercut the second long side of this triangle **22**. The second line does not go straight along the grain, but slightly rounds towards the base, so you need to stop the movement of the knife in the steepest curve of the triangle and, by changing the knife grip in your hand, finish cutting the side, starting from the base **23**, **24**.

Repeat all the steps on the remaining triangles in this section and in the section diagonally opposite, where the triangles also go along the grain **25**.

Next, carve a section of triangles that go against the grain. Undercut the longest triangle on the inside, starting from the top **26**. Next, cut the base of the triangle and then, by rotating the board, undercut the second long side. Find the steepest curve from the outside. Placing the knife at a 45-degree angle, start cutting the facet from this position **27**.

Once the undercut is made, change the knife grip in your hand, rotate the board, and undercut the rest of the facet to the base of the triangle, also starting from the steepest curve **28**. Finish carving all triangles in this section, and then in the section diagonally opposite, following the previous steps **29**.

Now cut the small straight-wall chips and the large ones for multi-level carving. Start with a small chip. Find the steepest curve in between the small and large ones. Hold the knife firmly at about 90 degrees to the surface of the board. Push the knife tip deep into the wood **30**.

25 Repeat all the steps on the remaining triangles and in the one section diagonally opposite, where the triangles also go along the grain.

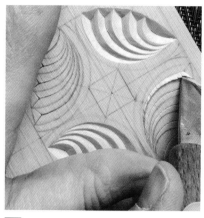

26 Undercut the longest triangle on the inside, starting from the top.

27 Place the knife at a 45-degree angle, and undercut the facet from the steepest curve.

28 Change the knife grip, rotate the board, and undercut the rest of the facet to the base of the triangle, starting from the steepest curve.

29 Finish carving all the triangles in this section, and then in the one diagonally opposite.

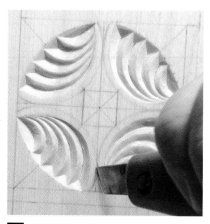

30 Push the tip of the knife deep into the wood.

31 Push the knife towards the intersecting corner of the small straight-wall sides to remove the chip.

32 Rotate the board and repeat all of these steps with a big straight-wall chip.

Repeat on the other side. Then lower the heel of the blade along the pencil line to the base of the triangle. Push the knife towards the intersecting corner of the straight-wall sides to remove the chip **31**. Rotate the board and repeat all these steps with a big straight-wall chip **32**, and then with the rest of the chips **33**.

To carve the smaller chips inside the large ones, stab the knife at an angle of almost 90 degrees, not to the surface of the board this time but to one of the large straight-wall chips instead. The movement of the inner smaller chips goes clockwise, so set the knife tip to the right side, 3–4mm from the top of the triangle by eye, then lower the heel to the base **34**, **35**. Repeat all the steps you made on the straight-wall chips to remove the smaller chips **36**.

The carving is now complete **37**.

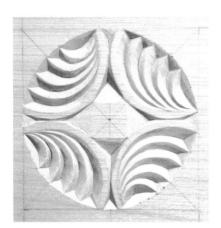

33 Carve the rest of the chips.

34 Set the knife tip to the right side 3–4mm from the top of the triangle by eye, then lower the heel to the base.

35 Repeat this on the other side.

36 Repeat all the steps on the straight-wall chips to remove the smaller chips.

37 The carving is now complete.

RHOMBUSES

As in the previous pattern, it will be necessary to change the knife grip in your hand several times when carving long rounded chips. But in this pattern these chips go along the grain so a slightly different undercutting technique can be used.

TOOLS AND MATERIALS

- BASSWOOD BOARD (AT LEAST 100–120MM SQUARE AND 15MM THICK)

- 0.5MM MECHANICAL PENCIL WITH H OR HB LEAD

- RULER

- COMPASS

- SKEW KNIFE

- SANDPAPER OR LEATHER STRIPS FOR SHARPENING

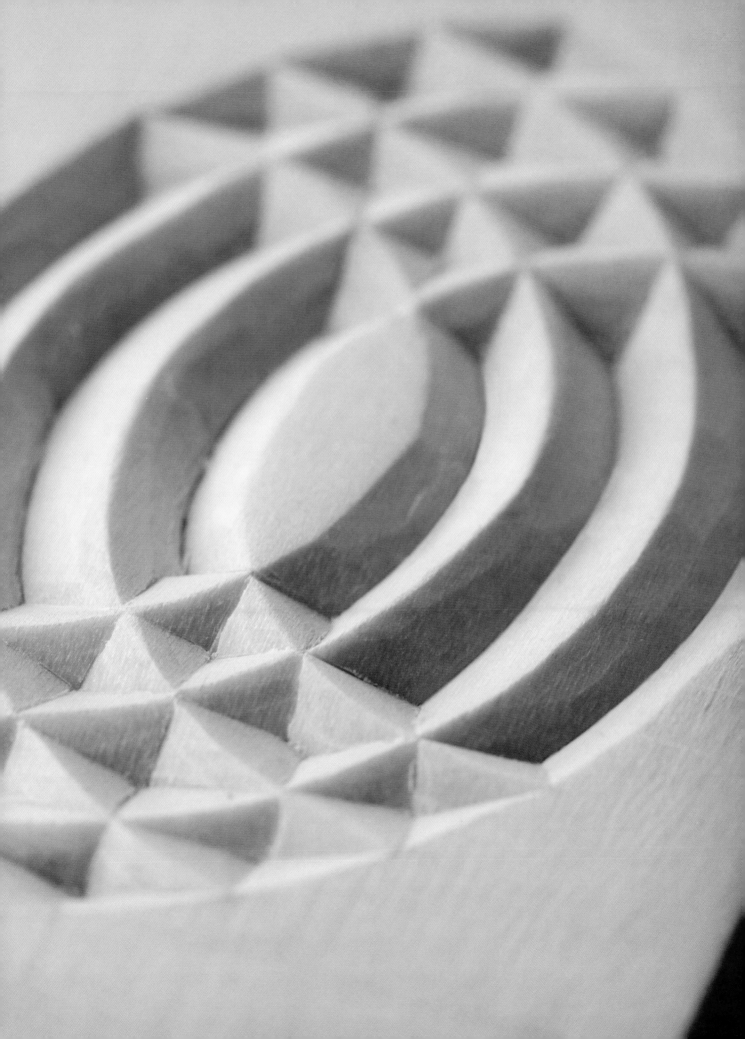

DRAWING PROCESS

If you would prefer to transfer this pattern to the basswood board, the template is on page 169, and guidelines on page 12. Otherwise, if you prefer to draw the pattern directly on to the basswood board, follow the instructions below.

First draw a rectangle 6cm long and 4cm wide. Then draw two perpendicular lines that intersect in the centre of the rectangle . Next, prepare an oval for the central and main pattern. Mark two dots 6mm from the top and bottom sides of the rectangle **2**. Place a compass on these dots, then draw curved lines **3**.

From the bottom previously prepared dot, mark two more dots 6mm from each other **4**. Place a compass on the opposite top dot, then draw three curved lines that will reach the opposite side of the oval, crossing the vertical perpendicular line (the radius of the first curved line crosses the first dot) **5**. Place a compass on the bottom dot (where one of the lines crossed it), and draw three curved lines on the opposite side, drawing them to the end, to the other side of the oval **6**.

1 Draw a rectangle with sides that are 6cm long and 4cm wide, then draw two perpendicular lines.

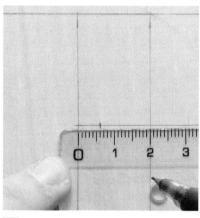

2 Mark two dots 6mm from the top and bottom sides of the rectangle.

3 Place a compass on the dots and draw two curved lines.

4 Mark two more dots 6mm from the bottom dot.

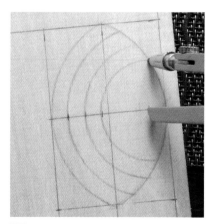

5 Draw three curved lines that reach the opposite side of the oval, crossing the vertical perpendicular line.

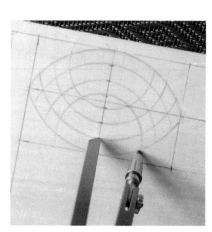

6 Place a compass on the bottom dot and draw three curved lines on the opposite side.

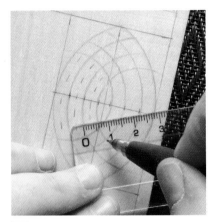

7 Now divide all of the four-sided chips in half.

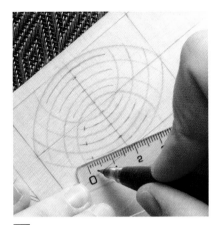

8 Mark dots 3mm from the bases of the four-sided chips.

Divide the resulting four-sided chips in half and then connect them together **7**.

Next, mark dots 3mm from the bases/short sides **8**, and connect them to the bases **9**. Now, in order to prepare the rhombuses for carving, connect all the tops of each rhombus with diagonal lines **10**.

The pattern is now ready for carving **11**.

9 Connect the dots with the bases.

10 Connect the tops of each rhombus with diagonal lines.

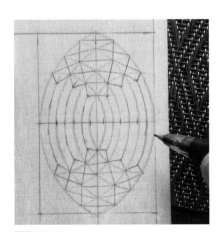

11 The pattern is drawn.

CARVING PROCESS

First, make all the stop cuts in all the rhombuses and four-sided chips **12**. When carving rhombuses in this pattern, you may need to employ the 'fake it till you make it' technique (see page 33). The rhombuses in this pattern consist of four triangles or four facets; you will need to carefully cut each facet of the rhombus so the knife tip does not go beyond one or other stop cut. To make this easier, cut each facet as if the task is to carve only this one, and the others do not exist.

Select any section with diamonds, to the right or left of the four-sided chips, and start cutting it from the inside, moving to the outside **13**. Each facet of a rhombus is undercut at an angle of approximately 60 degrees. When the first rhombus is done **14**, you can move from it first to the left, then to the right, and you will end up with a curved line of rhombuses **15**.

Continue in the same order until you finish carving the first section **16**.

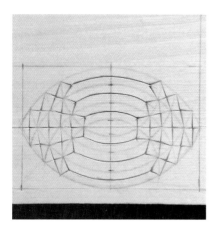

12 Make all the stop cuts in all the rhombuses and four-sided chips.

13 Start carving the rhombuses from the inside.

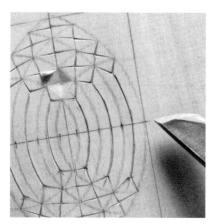

14 The first rhombus is done.

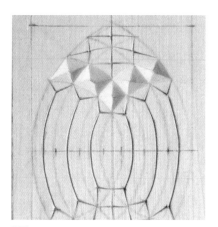

15 You will end up with a curved line of rhombuses when you carve the rhombuses from the left and right from the first one.

16 The first section of rhombuses is now done.

17 Start carving the second section of the rhombuses with the inner one.

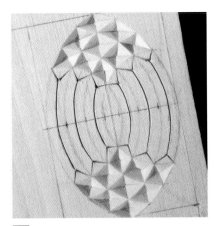

18 The second section of the rhombuses is done.

19 Carve the inner side of the first top four-sided chip, starting from the point where the perpendicular vertical line crosses it.

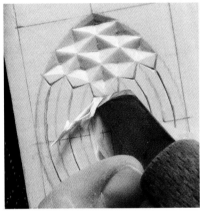

20 Change the knife grip and finish undercutting the first side of the first four-sided chip.

21 Begin to undercut the second long side, starting from the first short line and ending at the point where the perpendicular line goes.

22 Change the knife grip and finish cutting this side.

23 The first of the three top four-sided chips is complete.

Then proceed to the second section and cut it in the same order, starting with the inner rhombus **17** and ending with the outer **18**.

Now cut the central pattern, consisting of the top and bottom rows of four-sided chips. There are two techniques for undercutting the long sides of such patterns that go along the grain. You met the first one when you were carving out some of the previous patterns, where it was necessary to begin cutting the pattern from the steepest curve of the chip (see page 79, for example). You will carve the top four-sided chips using this same technique. Start carving the top chips from the inner chip, first cutting its inner side, starting from the point where the perpendicular vertical line crosses it **19**. Change the knife grip and finish cutting this side **20**.

Next, carve the short sides of the chip, then begin to undercut the second long side, starting from the first short line and ending at the point where the perpendicular line goes **21**. Change the knife grip and finish cutting this side **22**. The first of the three top four-sided chips is done **23**.

Now carve the rest of the three top four-sided chips, following the previous steps **24**.

Next, carve the bottom row of four-sided chips. Start with the inner chip and its inner side. Here you can use another technique for undercutting the sides. Place the knife about 4mm down from the perpendicular line. Start making an undercut from where the stop cut passes, without going beyond it **25**, then lead the knife to the stop cut near the short line **26**. Next, finish undercutting this side: set the knife about 4mm above the perpendicular line, and, again, start making an undercut from the place where the stop cut passes **27**. Lead the knife to the stop cut at the short line **28**.

I prefer this technique to the first one. It seems to offer more control over the undercutting of such curved sides. The second side of this chip is cut as well as on the top chips **29**.

24 Carve the rest of the four-sided chips, following the steps for carving the first top chip.

25 Place the knife about 4mm down from the perpendicular line, and start making an undercut where the stop cut passes.

26 Lead the knife to the stop cut near the short line.

27 Set the knife about 4mm above the perpendicular line, and start making the undercut.

28 Lead the knife to the stop cut at the short line.

29 The second side of this chip is cut as for the top chips.

30 The first bottom chip is complete.

31 Carve the second bottom chip, and its first long side, using the same technique.

When the first chip is complete **30**, go to the second lower chip using the same technique **31**. Once the second bottom chip is done **32**, carve out the remaining chips.

The carving is now complete **33**.

32 The second bottom chip is now complete.

33 The carving is now complete.

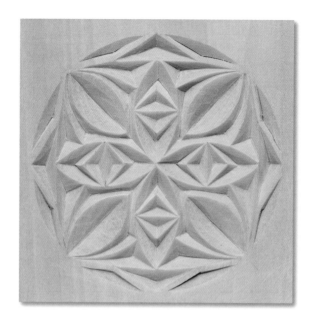

SNOWFLAKE

This pattern is slightly different from the previous ones, because it is completely filled with different chips. There are no empty spaces without carving (except for the thin gaps between external straight-wall chips and the rest of the pattern).

TOOLS AND MATERIALS

- BASSWOOD BOARD (AT LEAST 100–120MM SQUARE AND 15MM THICK)

- 0.5MM MECHANICAL PENCIL WITH H OR HB LEAD

- RULER

- COMPASS

- SKEW KNIFE

- SANDPAPER OR LEATHER STRIPS FOR SHARPENING

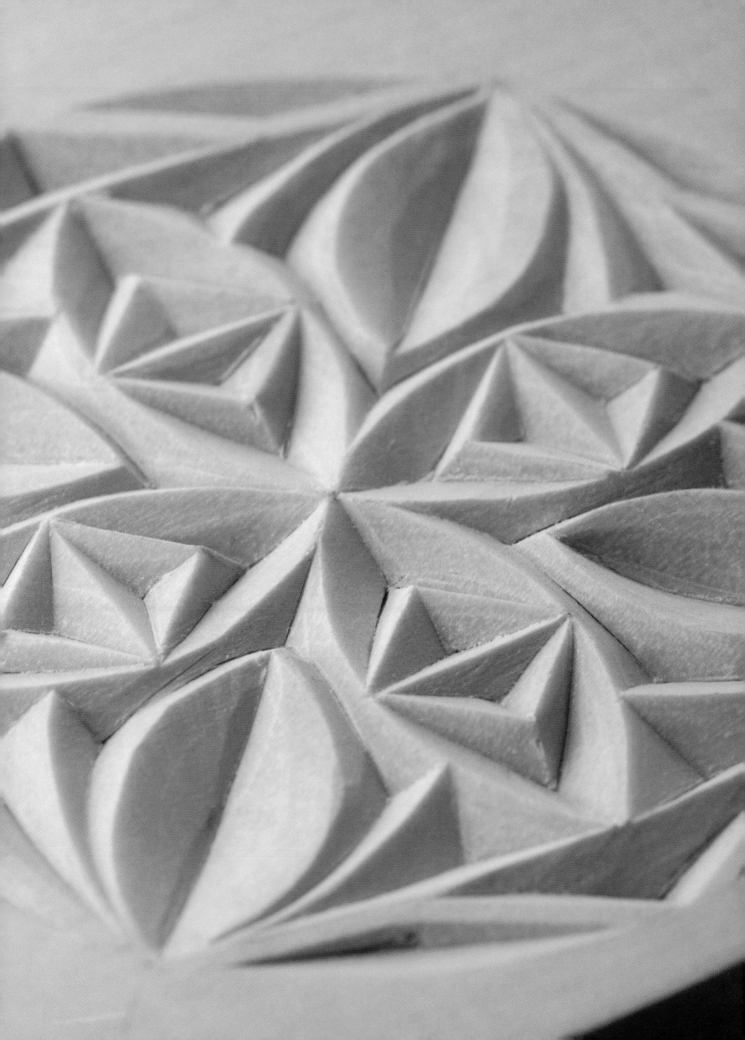

DRAWING PROCESS

If you would prefer to transfer this pattern to the basswood board, the template is on page 170, and guidelines on page 12. Otherwise, if you prefer to draw the pattern directly on to the basswood board, follow the instructions below.

First draw a square with the sides 7cm long. Then draw two perpendicular lines that intersect at the centre and two diagonal lines that connect the opposite corners of the square **1**.

Prepare a circle for the central and main pattern. Using a compass, draw a circle with a 3.5cm radius inside the square. Mark dots on the diagonal lines 2cm from the centre of the pattern **2**. Place the compass on the dots and draw semicircles **3**.

Next, find the dots to draw other sharp ovals in each quarter of the square and between the previously drawn ovals. To do this, step 1.5cm away from the point where the vertical perpendicular line divides the top side of the square in half and draw a short line to the left of the perpendicular line approximately in the middle of the section **4**. Next, mark a short line 2.5cm from the centre that crosses the first one **5**. Place the compass at the intersection of these short lines and draw a curved line to form one side of the future oval to the left of the point (that is, anticlockwise) **6**.

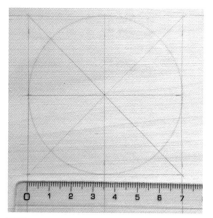

1 Draw a square with 7cm-long sides and two diagonal and perpendicular lines. Draw a circle with a 3.5cm radius inside the square.

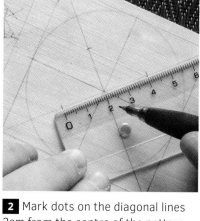

2 Mark dots on the diagonal lines 2cm from the centre of the pattern.

3 Place the compass on the dots and draw semicircles.

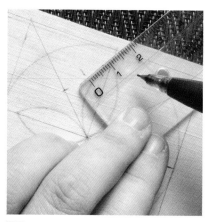

4 Draw a short line to the left of the perpendicular line approximately in the middle of the section.

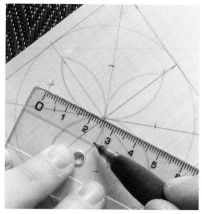

5 Mark a short line 2.5cm from the centre that crosses the first one.

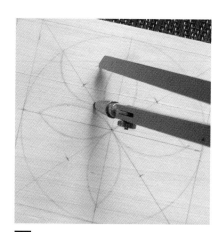

6 Place the compass at the intersection of the lines and draw a curved line.

7 Mark the remaining dots.

8 Draw the remaining curved lines.

Next, mark the remaining dots following the steps taken to find the first dot **7**, and draw the remaining curved lines **8**.

Now designate the space around these ovals, for this purpose inside the central ovals, where the perpendicular lines pass, and mark a dot 2.1cm from the centre of the pattern **9**. Place the compass on these dots, and draw curved lines in the two quarters of the square that are next to each other **10**. Draw the lines through the dots that were prepared for the ovals that go between the central ovals. Next, position the compass on the remaining three dots and draw the other curved lines **11**.

9 Mark a dot 2.1cm from the centre of the pattern.

10 Place the compass on the dots and draw curved lines.

11 Place the compass on the remaining three dots and draw the other curved lines.

Now draw triangles for the straight-wall chips that go around the perimeter of the circle. Divide each section of the circle in half, mark a short line **12**, then measure 5mm on this short line starting from the line of the circle – this will be the tip of the future chip **13**. Connect this dot with those points that limit the section of the circle **14**. Using a dotted line, mark 1mm from the received line **15** and connect them together.

Repeat these steps to draw triangles for straight-wall chips in the remaining sections and also thick lines to separate the chips from the main pattern **16**.

Now connect the apex of the triangle for a straight-wall chip with the top of the oval using a ruler to delimit this space for another triangle **17**.

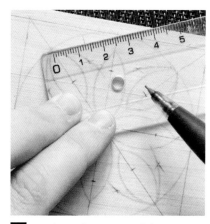

12 Divide each section of the circle in half.

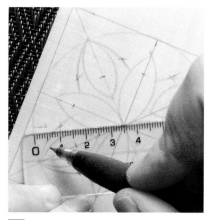

13 Measure 5mm on this short line, starting from the line of the circle.

14 Connect the dot with the base of the triangle.

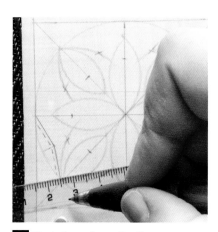

15 Mark 1mm from the line.

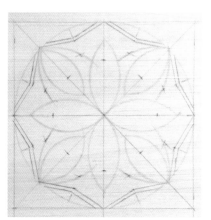

16 Repeat all the steps to draw triangles for straight-wall chips and also thick lines to separate the chips from the main pattern.

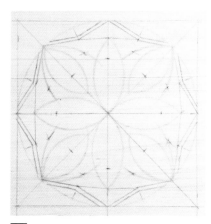

17 Connect the apex of the triangle for a straight-wall chip with the top of the oval.

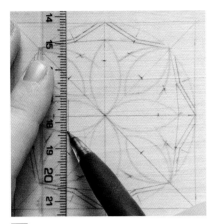

18 Draw a line inside one oval.

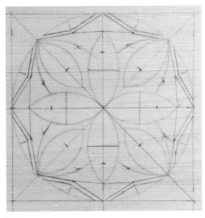

19 Then draw lines inside all the other ovals.

Next, draw rhombuses inside the central ovals. Using a ruler, connect the dots that were prepared in order to draw the central ovals. First, on one side (for example, the left), draw a line inside the oval **18**, and then on the top, the right and on the bottom **19**. Now mark dots 6mm to the right and left of the received lines **20**, and connect them to the base/perpendicular line that divided the rhombus in half. Further on, we will designate triangles/find lines for additional undercutting.

Now draw lines for additional stop cuts: mark 2mm to the right and left of the perpendicular line inside the rhombuses **21**, and connect them to a common base of triangles.

The pattern is now ready for carving **22**.

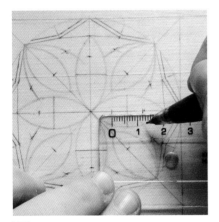

20 Mark dots 6mm to the right and left of the lines.

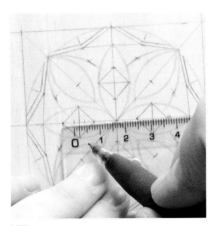

21 Mark 2mm to the right and left of the perpendicular line inside the rhombuses.

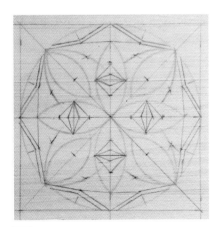

22 The pattern is drawn.

CARVING PROCESS

First, make all the stop cuts in all the chips of the pattern. The only place where you won't make them for now is around the rhombuses in the central ovals, since you will cut these rhombuses first, and any undercutting is not necessary at the moment **23**.

Begin to cut the first rhombuses that go along the grain. Each facet of the triangles is undercut at an angle of 45 degrees. For example, start cutting the bottom rhombus and the bottom triangle. Try and see when the knife goes smoothly and without chipping along the grain **24**, **25**. Then go to the upper triangle and cut it **26**, **27**.

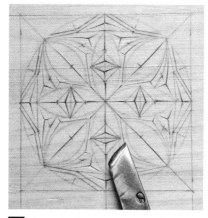

23 Make all the stop cuts in the chips of the pattern except around the rhombuses in the central ovals.

24 Start cutting the bottom rhombus and the bottom triangle inside it.

25 The first triangle is complete.

26 Carve the second triangle inside the rhombus.

FOLLOW THE SEQUENCE

As you might have noticed, this pattern seems complicated at first glance, but if you follow the carving steps sequentially, holding the knife correctly in your hand and at the right angles, carving becomes a joy and everything goes much easier.

27 The second triangle is done.

28 Lead the knife along the whole side of the rhombus.

29 Carve the sides of the triangles without bases at an angle of about 65 degrees.

Once the first rhombus has been cut, start cutting its sides from the outside at an angle of about 65 degrees, placing the tip of the knife 1mm to the right beyond the perpendicular line. Since the apex of the rhombus is the deepest point, first push the knife deep into the wood; then, without taking it out of the wood, slide the knife along the entire side of the rhombus, carefully leading it to the place where the base of the triangle would be **28**.

Repeat these steps on the other sides of the rhombus. Then cut the sides of the triangles without bases, which, together with the rhombus, form the oval, at an angle of about 65 degrees **29**. The first central oval is complete **30**. Repeat these steps on the opposite oval **31**.

Next, carve the two central rhombuses and ovals **32**, **33**.

30 The first central oval is done.

31 Carve the second oval and the rhombus inside of it.

32 Start carving the next two central rhombuses and ovals.

33 This stage is complete.

The next task is to carve out the spaces around those rhombuses that go between the central ones. Make sure your knife is still sharp; if not, sharpen it on sandpaper or leather strips (see page 10): when undercutting the spaces, you need the tip of the knife and this has to be sharp. Following the direction of the grain and changing the knife grip in your hand, carefully cut the space at an angle of 65 degrees, without going beyond the stop cuts **34**.

When you have finished cutting the first space, start cutting the oval inside it. To simplify the task of carving these large ovals or double-sided chips, first you can remove a smaller chip inside the big one **35**, then carve the entire side completely **36**. Repeat these steps on the other side of the chip **37**. If the chips do not pop out, either repeat the stop cut or undercut the sides at the same angle **38**. Then cut the spaces around the remaining ovals and the ovals themselves **39**.

34 Carefully cut the space around the ovals at an angle of 65 degrees.

35 Remove a smaller chip inside the big one.

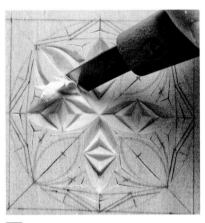

36 Carve the entire side completely.

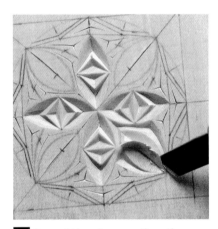

37 Repeat the steps on the other side of the chip.

38 If the chips do not pop out, either repeat the stop cut or undercut the sides at the same angle.

39 Cut the spaces around the remaining ovals and the ovals themselves.

40 Undercut the sides of the triangles that are connected to the already carved pattern.

41 Carve out the remaining triangles.

42 Carve the straight-wall chips around the main pattern by changing the knife grip in your hand.

43 The carving is now complete.

Now carve the triangles around the already carved pattern, and then the straight-wall chips. First, undercut those sides of the triangles that are connected and, in some sense, are common with the already carved pattern. Then trim the long sides, which here also act as the bases of the triangles **40**. Carve out the remaining triangles, following my method of carving the sides along the grain where necessary **41**.

Now carve the straight-wall chips. They are made as usual straight-wall chips, only here they go in different directions along the grain, which means you need to change the knife grip in your hand every time **42**.

The carving is now complete **43**.

SWIRL

This multi-level pattern might seem complex at first glance, but it consists only of long, slightly curved straight-walled chips connected to each other and smaller chips carved inside them.

TOOLS AND MATERIALS

- BASSWOOD BOARD (AT LEAST 100–120MM SQUARE AND 15MM THICK)

- 0.5MM MECHANICAL PENCIL WITH H OR HB LEAD

- RULER

- COMPASS

- SKEW KNIFE

- SANDPAPER OR LEATHER STRIPS FOR SHARPENING

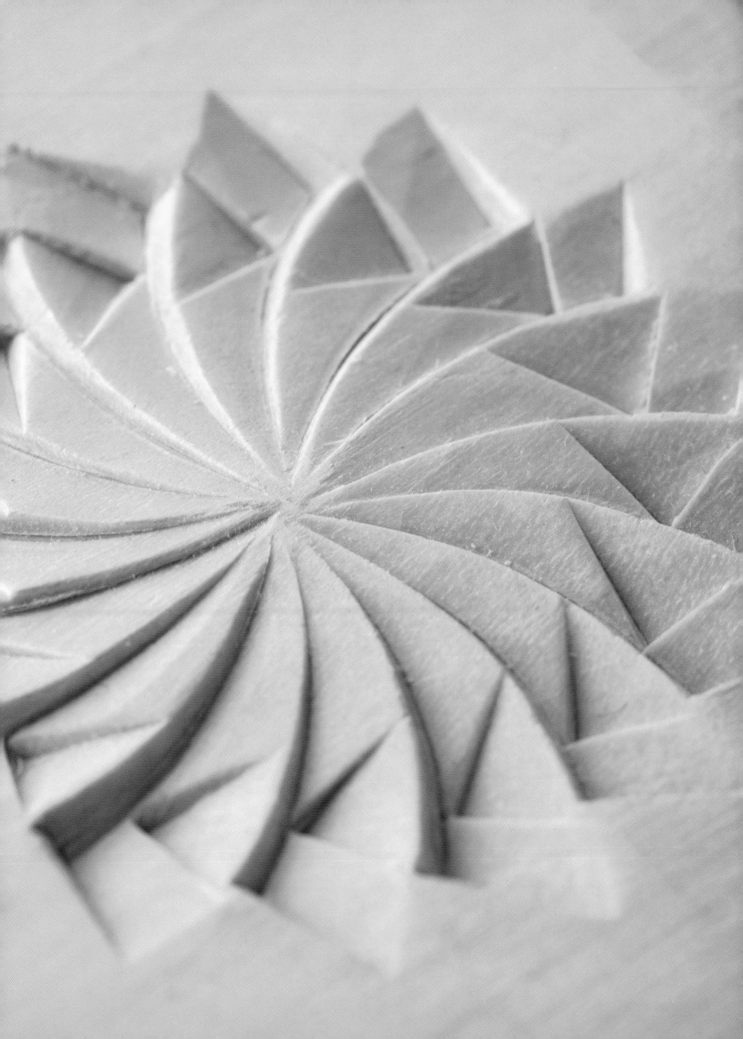

DRAWING PROCESS

If you would prefer to transfer this pattern to the basswood board, the template is on page 170, and guidelines on page 12. Otherwise, if you prefer to draw the pattern directly on to the basswood board, follow the instructions below.

First draw a square with the sides 5cm long. Then draw two perpendicular lines that intersect at the centre and two diagonal lines that connect the opposite corners of the square.

Next, prepare a circle for the central and main pattern. Using a compass, draw a 2.5cm-radius circle inside the square **1**. Divide each of the eight sections of the circle in half. Put dots instead of drawing lines inside the circle in order not to confuse the lines when carving **2**.

Next, measure a radius of 2.5cm and, placing a compass on each of the dots, draw curved lines **3**. In order to achieve a stronger 'swirl' effect, mark dots 6mm from the circle on each of the lines **4**. To save time, mark a dot on one of the lines and make the rest using a compass **5**.

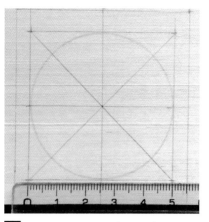

1 Draw a square with 5cm-long sides and two diagonal and perpendicular lines. Draw a circle with a 3.5cm radius inside the square.

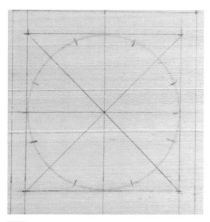

2 Divide each section of the circle in half.

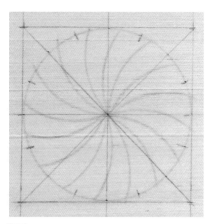

3 Place a compass on the dots, and draw the curved lines.

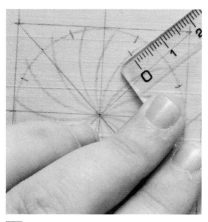

4 Mark dots 6mm from the circle on each of the curved lines.

5 Mark dots on each line using a compass.

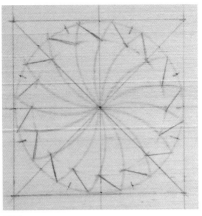

The movement of the spiral goes clockwise, so begin to draw short lines by hand, starting from the top of the line to the previously prepared dots **6**, **7**.

The pattern is ready for carving.

6 Connect the top of the lines with the prepared dots by hand.

7 The pattern is drawn.

CARVING PROCESS

Start carving this pattern with a chip next to the one that goes along the grain. When you are finishing the carving of a swirl, it will be easier to remove/carve the last chip without chipping or breaking the next one. Do not undercut all the straight-wall chips at once. Make two cuts for one straight-wall chip, then undercut it; make two cuts for

the next chip, then undercut it, and so on. All the undercuts of the chips go clockwise from the first chip. Thus, an undercut will never be done on an already carved chip, except for the last one, but since the undercut will go along the grain no problems should arise.

Make cuts on both sides of the chip – on the long one, which

partially shares one long side with the next chip, and on the short side of the chip – at 90 degrees to the surface of the wood. The deepest knife pressure is where the intersecting corner is **8**. Rotate the board so it is convenient for you to cut the chip. Following the grain, carve it as if you were cutting a simple straight-wall chip **9**, **10**.

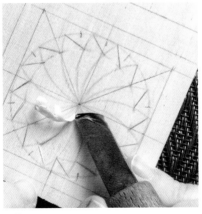

8 Make cuts on both sides of the first chip – the long and the short – at an angle of 90 degrees to the surface of the wood.

9 Rotate the board and carve a chip as a simple straight-wall chip.

10 The first chip is done.

Start making cuts for the second chip again from the side that is partly shared with the next chip **11**.

All undercuts to the chip, which is directly on the perpendicular vertical line in this quarter of the pattern, go away from you **12**. The next undercuts of the chips, starting with the one that is located beyond the perpendicular line, in the next quarter of the pattern, are already done towards you **13**. So, in order not to get confused about how to hold the knife and undercut the chip in one way or another, just be sure about how one chip is cut in each quarter of the pattern, and the rest will be cut in the same way. Carve the remaining chips **14**.

Next, using a pencil, draw lines by eye parallel to the short sides of the triangles, which end at the deepest point on the short line and where it crosses the long side of the next chip **15**. Make a cut at a 90-degree angle to the surface of the carved chip, then mark a dot 7mm below, starting from the point where the previous cut ended **16**. Put a dot on the long side of the chip and then, from the beginning of the previous cut, at the intersecting corner, make a cut, as for a straight-wall chip, at a 90-degree angle **17**.

11 Start cutting the second chip.

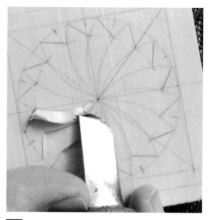

12 Finish carving the first quarter of the circle.

13 Start carving the next quarter of the circle by changing the knife grip.

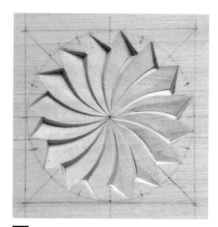

14 The first stage of carving the pattern is complete.

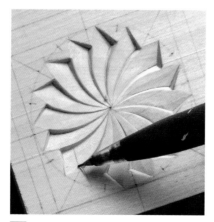

15 Draw lines parallel to the short sides of the triangles by eye using a pencil.

16 Mark a dot 7mm below, starting from the point where the previous cut ended.

17 Make a cut as for a straight-wall chip at a 90-degree angle at the intersecting corner.

18 Repeat these cuts on the remaining chips.

Repeat these steps on the remaining chips **18**. Then, keeping the knife grip the same as when undercutting the main chips in each quarter of the circle, carve the small chips, pushing the knife towards the intersecting corners **19**, **20**.

The carving is now complete **21**.

19 Carve the small chips, pushing the knife towards the intersecting corners.

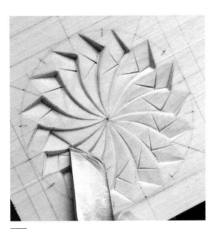

20 The first small chip is done.

21 The carving is now complete.

KALEIDOSCOPE

The carving of this pattern, like the next two, is done without stop cuts. In this more challenging piece, there are multi-level patterns connected to each other in the centre, continuous thin lines and complex chips going around the main sections.

TOOLS AND MATERIALS

- BASSWOOD BOARD (AT LEAST 100–120MM SQUARE AND 15MM THICK)

- 0.5MM MECHANICAL PENCIL WITH H OR HB LEAD

- RULER

- COMPASS

- SKEW KNIFE

- SANDPAPER OR LEATHER STRIPS FOR SHARPENING

- LONG NAIL AND HAMMER (OPTIONAL)

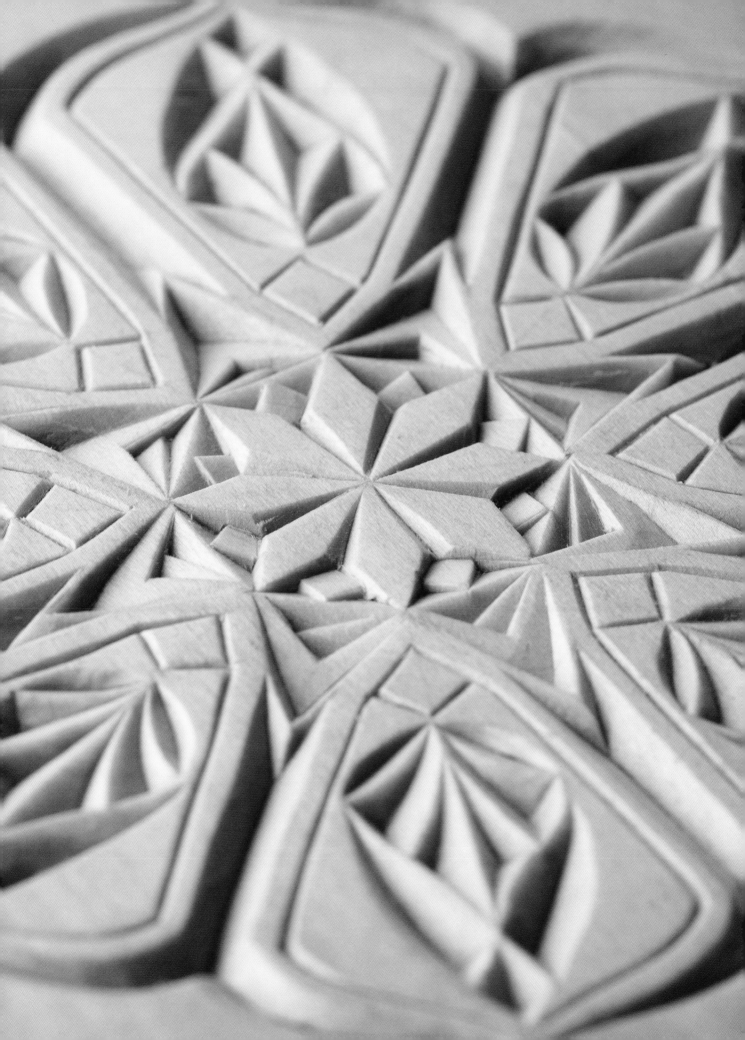

DRAWING PROCESS

If you would prefer to transfer this pattern to the basswood board, the template is on page 170, and guidelines on page 12. Otherwise, if you prefer to draw the pattern directly on to the basswood board, follow the instructions below.

First draw a square with the sides 14cm long. Then draw two perpendicular lines that intersect at the centre and two diagonal lines that connect the opposite corners of the square **1**. Stepping 7mm from any side of the square **2**, use a compass to draw a circle with a radius of 6.3cm **3**. Draw two small circles inside this large one, with radiuses of 1.5cm and 2.4cm **4**.

To mark the sections of this pattern, first, at the top of the large circle, mark dots 2mm to the right and left of the central line **5**. At the top of the middle circle, mark dots 3mm on the right and left sides of the central line **6**.

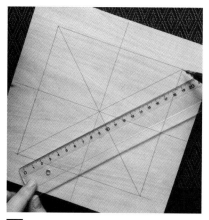

1 Draw a square that has 14cm-long sides, then draw two perpendicular and two diagonal lines.

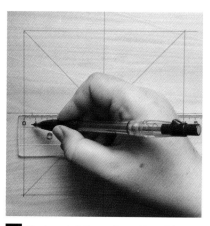

2 Mark a dot 7mm from the side of the square.

3 Using a compass, draw a 6.3cm-radius circle.

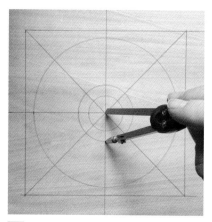

4 Draw two more circles inside the first one.

5 Mark dots 2mm on the right and left sides from the central line.

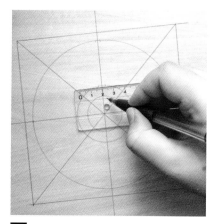

6 Mark dots 3mm on the right and left sides of the central line at the top point of the middle circle.

7 Divide a section of the smallest circle in half, marking a dot and connecting the formed sides of the pattern below together.

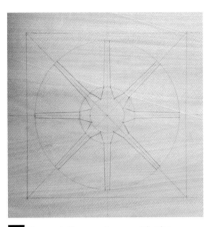

8 Repeat these steps with the remaining sections.

Connect the dots on the right side together, then connect the dots on the left side. Divide the smallest circle in half, mark a dot and connect together the formed sides of the section below **7**. Repeat this in the remaining sections **8**. Divide all the prepared sections in half and connect them to the centre of the pattern **9**.

Starting from the outer sides of the sections, draw short lines parallel to the sides of the sections at 5mm intervals **10**. Starting with the line closest to the side of the section, mark a dot on it 5.6cm from the centre of the pattern **11**. Place a second dot on the second line 5.8cm from the centre **12**.

9 Divide the main sections of the pattern in half and, using a ruler, connect them to the centre of the pattern with straight lines.

10 Draw short lines parallel to the sides of the sections at 5mm intervals, starting from the outer sides of the sections.

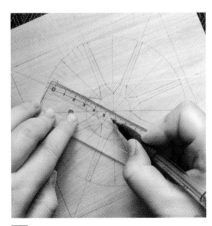

11 Mark the first dot 5.6cm from the centre of the pattern, starting with the first line that is closest to the side of the section.

12 Mark the second dot on the second line 5.8cm from the centre.

Make a third dot on the third line closest to the central line of the section 5.9cm from the centre of the pattern **13**. On the section's sides, mark the dots or draw a short line 5.2cm from the centre **14**. Smoothly connect all the dots together **15**.

Repeat these steps inside the remaining sections **16**.

On the diagonal and central lines of the entire pattern, mark dots on the right and left sides of the main pattern sections 5.6cm from the centre of the pattern **17**. Measure 5mm from the 'shoulder' of the pattern inside the section and place a dot there **18**. Then, repeating the contours of the pattern, draw a smooth line to connect with the highest point of the pattern inside the section **19**.

13 Mark the third dot on the third line closest to the central line of the section 5.9cm from the centre of the pattern.

14 Mark short lines 5.2cm on the section's sides starting from the centre.

15 Smoothly connect up the dots.

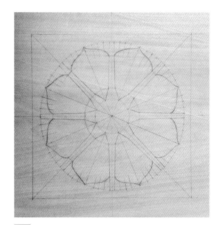

16 The shapes of the main sections are done.

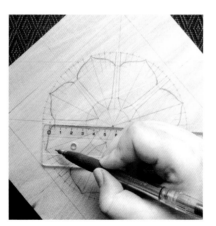

17 Mark the dots on the diagonal and central lines of the pattern, on the right and left sides of the main sections.

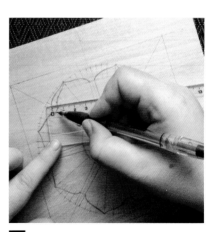

18 Measure 5mm from the 'shoulder', or the most curved place and put a dot there.

19 Draw a smooth line, repeating the contours of the shoulder of the section.

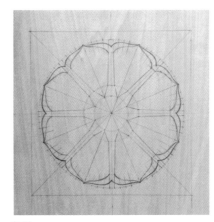

20 Repeat this with the other remaining sections.

Repeat these steps in the remaining sections **20**.

Now move to the internal drawing of each section. Step 2mm from the sides of the section, mark short lines or dots 5–10mm from each other **21**, then connect them together **22** to form the contours of the pattern for line carving. To draw a rhombus at the bottom of the section, mark a dot on the central line of the section 8mm from the line you just made for line carving **23**. Draw two lines from this dot to connect with those dots made by crossing the inner lines for line carving and the middle circle of the entire pattern **24**. Continue to fill the sections with details.

To draw the semicircle, mark a dot on the central line of the section 3.6cm from the centre of the pattern. Measure a radius of 1.6cm and draw a shape slightly bigger than a semicircle **25**.

21 Mark short lines 2mm from the sides of the section and 5–10mm from each other.

22 Connect them together.

23 Mark a dot on the central line of the section 8mm from the inner line.

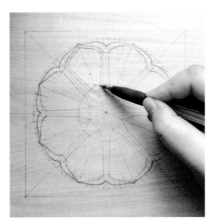

24 Draw two lines from the dot, connecting it with the dots on the inner line.

25 Draw a little more than a semicircle inside the section.

Place a compass at the highest point of the central line of the entire pattern, to the right of the section you have just drawn, measure a radius of 3.3cm, and mark a short line on one of the semicircle sides **26**. Place the compass on the top point of the circle where there is a diagonal line of the entire pattern, to the left of the section, and on the other side of the semicircle **27**. To make a 'raindrop' shape out of the semicircle, mark a dot 5.1cm from the centre **28** on the central line of the section, and smoothly connect the semicircle to this point **29**. Mark a dot 4.4cm on the central line of the entire pattern, to the right side of the section **30**.

Place the compass on this dot, having previously measured a radius of 2.5cm, and draw a curved line to the left side of a raindrop **31**. Repeat this on the other side.

26 Measure a radius of 3.3cm and mark a short line on one of the semicircle sides.

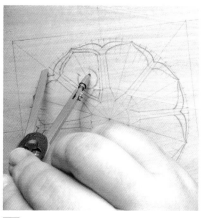

27 Mark the other side of the semicircle by placing the compass on the point where the circle crosses the diagonal line.

28 Mark a dot 5.1cm on the central line of the section, starting from the centre of the pattern.

29 Connect the dot with the semicircle.

30 Mark a dot 4.4cm on the central line of the entire pattern.

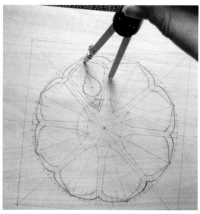

31 Place a compass on the dot and draw a curved line on the left of the pattern.

32 Mark dots 5mm on the left and right sides of the pattern inside the section, starting from the top.

33 Draw a curved line from the bottom to the right side of a raindrop shape.

34 Mark a dot on the right side of a raindrop 3.5cm from the centre.

35 Connect the dot with the bottom of the pattern.

To finish drawing this and the other sections, from the common top of the newly formed curved lines, mark dots 5mm on the left and right sides **32**. To fill a raindrop with triangles, draw a smooth curve from the bottom to the right side of a raindrop to the short line that we prepared to draw a raindrop **33**. The first triangle is done. Position the compass at the centre of the entire pattern, having previously measured a radius of 3.5cm, and mark a dot or short line on the right side of a raindrop **34**. Smoothly connect it with the bottom of a raindrop **35**.

Repeat these steps on the other side of a raindrop of this section **36**. Then repeat all the steps that you have done in this section inside all the other sections **37**.

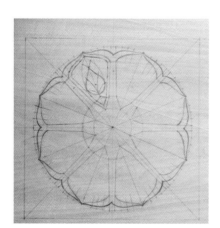

36 Finish drawing the other side of the pattern.

37 The main sections of the pattern are completely drawn.

Now start drawing the central small pattern – a star shape in which there is multi-level carving. Mark a dot on the diagonal line of the entire pattern 8mm from the centre **38**. Place the compass at the centre of the pattern and mark dots or short lines through one line from the first dot **39**. Connect all the dots with the bases of the patterns in the sections **40**. Connect all the apexes of the star with straight lines **41**. To prepare triangles for multi-level carving, mark dots on all central and diagonal lines of the pattern 3cm from the centre **42**. Then draw lines from these dots and connect them with the apexes of the star **43**.

38 Mark a dot 8mm from the centre on the diagonal line of the entire pattern.

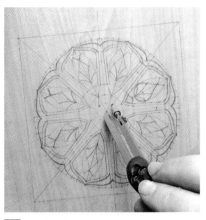

39 Mark a dot on every other line.

40 Connect the dots with the bases of the patterns.

41 Connect the apexes of the star together with straight lines.

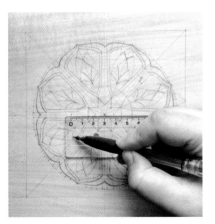

42 Mark dots on all central and diagonal lines of the pattern 3cm from the centre.

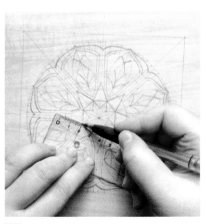

43 Connect the dots with the apexes of the star.

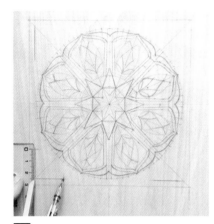

44 Draw lines 2.5cm long in the corners of the pattern.

45 Start connecting the ends of these lines together.

46 Mark dots 1cm from each end of the lines.

47 Mark a dot 5mm from the outer circle of the pattern.

48 Place a compass on the dot and draw a curved line.

49 The pattern is drawn.

You can decorate the pattern with hammering or skip this step and proceed to carving. To prepare the corners of the pattern for hammering, step 5mm from the sides of a square and draw lines 2.5cm long **44**. Start connecting the ends of these lines together, but do not connect them in the middle of the diagonal line of the pattern **45**. Step 1cm from each end of the lines and mark dots **46**. Then step back 5mm from the largest circle and mark a dot **47**. Place a compass on this dot, having previously measured a radius of 1cm, and draw almost a semicircle **48**. Repeat these steps on all four corners.

The pattern is now ready for carving **49**.

CARVING PROCESS

The carving of this pattern, like the next two patterns, is done without stop cuts. This image (**50**) shows the pattern in the top left quarter of the design. This requires carving a) against the grain, b) along the grain, and c) carving the patterns in different directions. Before you start carving the main sections of the pattern and the patterns inside them, carve out the spaces around each section. First, work on the space around the section that goes along the grain. The first cut starts where there is an abrupt transition from a 'shoulder' of the pattern, and where the knife changes direction it is necessary to change the knife grip **51**.

Move to the triangle inside this carving-out space **52**, then change the knife grip and cut a shoulder of the pattern inside the section **53** and the top line above it **54**. Repeat all the movements on the other side of the carving-out space, following the direction of the grain (all movements of the knife will be mirrored: if on the first side you held the knife towards yourself, on the other side you hold it away from you). Then cut the sides of the triangle, but step up a bit, mentally tracing up the side of the triangle. At the top the cutting movement is quite insignificant, and the tip of the knife should only go a little way into the wood, so as not to leave a mark from the knife on the side of the section, but where the facets of the triangle meet, there you can make the deepest incision of the knife **55**.

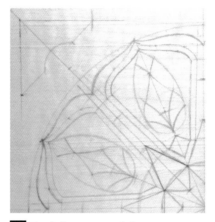

50 Top left quarter of the pattern.

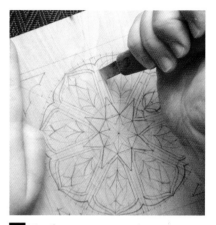

51 The first cut starts where there is an abrupt transition from a 'shoulder' of the pattern.

52 Lead the knife to the triangle.

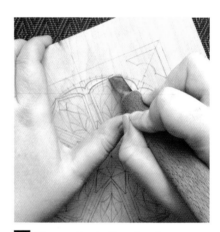

53 Change the knife grip when cutting the shoulder of the pattern.

54 Change the knife grip again to cut the top side, repeating the contours of the section.

55 Carefully cut the sides of the triangle inside the cutting-out space.

56 Repeat the undercuts until the chip pops out.

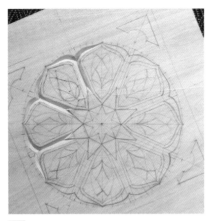

57 Carve out the remaining sections in this quarter of the pattern.

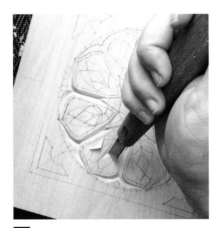

58 Start carving the pattern inside the section.

59 Finish carving the first chip.

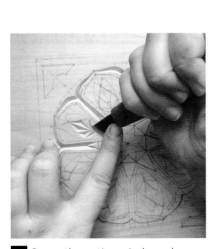

60 Carve the entire raindrop shape.

If, after all this, the chip has not popped out, then repeat all the cutting movements until it pops out **56**.

Next, cut the two remaining spaces around the sections with the main patterns, following the direction of the grain. In these cases, it is better to start by cutting the triangles inside the carving-out spaces, so that the faces of the triangles do not break, as these carving-out spaces go against the grain or have different directions on the wood **57**.

Now return to the first section of the main pattern, which mainly goes along the grain, and begin to carve a raindrop shape. When carving a raindrop, it is better to start with the triangles/chips inside it that are next to each other and connected by bases **58**, **59**.

Next, carve out those triangles/chips that go under them, one after another, to better control their carving. It is important to keep to this sequence of steps rather than randomly carving chips **60**.

Now carve out the big chips around a raindrop. The first cut needs to be done next to what was already carved inside a raindrop. Very carefully, cut the top of the chip at the bottom of a raindrop to the top of a raindrop itself – almost effortlessly at first, but pushing the knife deeper by the end **61**, **62**.

Now you need to carve out the rhombus. Begin to cut it from the sides next to what has already been carved out **63**, **64**.

Finish this section by carving out the line: begin to cut the line from the inside, because the composition with a raindrop is very close to it, and you will need to follow it carefully so as not to break it **65**. Cut the line along the entire perimeter from the inside **66**. Then start cutting the line from the outside **67**, **68**.

61 Start carving the chip around a raindrop at a 45-degree angle.

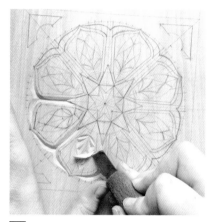

62 Finish carving the chip, also at a 45-degree angle.

63 Carve the rhombus at the top of the pattern starting from the sides that are next to what has already been carved out.

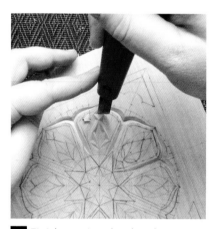

64 Finish carving the rhombus.

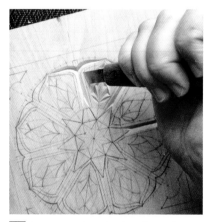

65 Begin cutting the line from the inside, starting from the shoulder.

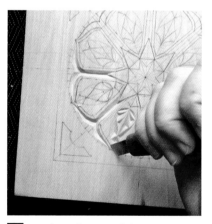

66 Finish at the top of the pattern.

67 Finish carving the line from the outside.

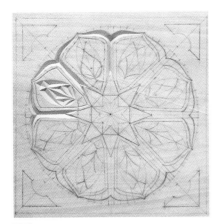

68 The line is carved.

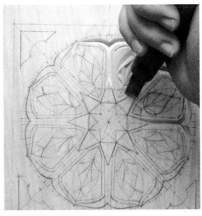

69 Cut a rhombus at the bottom, first from the inside and then from the outside.

There is a rhombus at the base of the section; cut it first from the inside, and then from the outside **69**, **70**. The first section is carved out; now carve the second one. Begin by cutting the chips that are inside a raindrop **71**, as you did in the first section, then the big chips around a raindrop **72**, then a rhombus **73**, and then the line carving **74**.

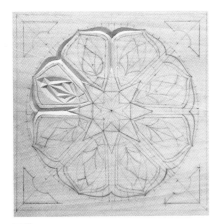

70 The first section is carved completely.

71 Start carving the section from the chips that are inside a raindrop.

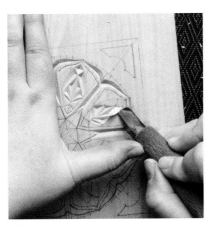

72 Carve the big chips around a raindrop.

73 Next, carve a rhombus at the top of the pattern.

74 Finish carving the section with a line around the raindrop.

Now move to carving out the central pattern, where there is only multi-level carving. Begin by carving out the triangles in the centre that go along the grain. Raise the knife right above the first side of the chip, then push the tip of the knife to the top of the triangles, where the facets meet, at an angle of almost 90 degrees. Then, by not removing the knife from the wood, do the same on the other side. Now turn the board away from you (35–45 degrees) so that you can lay the knife blade low to the wood along the third side of the chip (the short side of your isosceles triangle), and push the knife towards the intersecting corner of the straight-wall sides (the apex of the triangle) . To carve the smaller chip inside this chip, stab the knife at an angle of almost 90 degrees – not to the surface of the board this time, but to the surface of the big chip instead. Repeat all the steps you made on the straight-wall chips to remove a smaller chip .

Carve another triangle inside this small chip. To do that, repeat the steps as for the rest of the straight-wall chips, but start on one side of the small chip rather than in the middle . Once this multi-level straight-wall chip is done, carve out the opposite one . Then carve a rhombus inside this chip. To do this, repeat the steps to carve out a small chip inside a big one. Mentally divide a big straight-wall chip in half and, starting from the left side, make a cut; make one on the opposite side of the triangle too.

75 Push the knife towards the intersecting corner of the straight-wall sides to remove it.

76 Carve a smaller chip inside the big chip.

77 Then carve one even smaller chip inside the second small chip.

78 Carve out the opposite straight-wall chip.

79 Then carve two smaller chips inside of it.

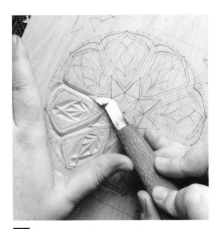

80 Carve out the remaining straight-wall chips, following the grain direction.

81 Make cuts to highlight the central star at an angle of 35–40 degrees.

82 Take a long nail and a hammer for hammering.

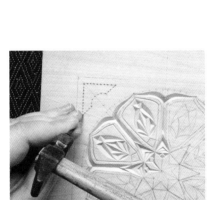

83 Make dots around the entire perimeter of the shape.

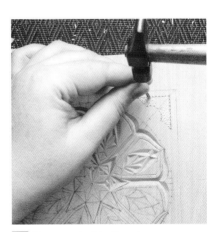

84 Hammer inside the shape.

85 The carving is now complete.

Then, by turning the board, repeat these steps and cut these small straight-wall chips as you did to remove the small straight-wall chips in the previous big one **79**. Carve the remaining triangles using the same steps **80**.

To finish this quarter of the pattern, make cuts to highlight the central star. Place the knife about 1mm away from the line that runs through the centre of the multi-level triangles. Make cuts at an angle of almost 35–40 degrees on one side and then the other side of the line, but avoid cutting to the centre of the pattern **81**. Repeat these steps on the other lines.

The next step, hammering the corners of the pattern, is optional. If you want to do it, you will need a long nail and a hammer **82**. To hammer the shape that we prepared during the drawing process, put a nail on the drawn line of a shape and hit it with the hammer. Make dots along the entire perimeter **83**, and then hammer inside the shape **84**.

You have carved out one quarter of the entire pattern. Now repeat the carving steps in the other three quarters.

The carving is now complete **85**.

WOODEN WINDOW

The main shapes in this pattern are the petals and the connecting triangles within them. Two thin rectangles frame the central pattern at the top and bottom, filled with multi-level carving.

TOOLS AND MATERIALS

- BASSWOOD BOARD (AT LEAST 100–120MM SQUARE AND 15MM THICK)

- 0.5MM MECHANICAL PENCIL WITH H OR HB LEAD

- RULER

- COMPASS

- SKEW KNIFE

- SANDPAPER OR LEATHER STRIPS FOR SHARPENING

DRAWING PROCESS

If you would prefer to transfer this pattern to the basswood board, the template is on page 171, and guidelines on page 12. Otherwise, if you prefer to draw the pattern directly on to the basswood board, follow the instructions below.

First draw a rectangle 13.7cm long and 10.2cm wide. Then draw two perpendicular lines that intersect at the centre of the rectangle **1**.

Next, delimit the rectangle so that the centre has a square for the main pattern: mark dots 5.1cm from the vertical perpendicular line, from below and from above, to the left and to the right of it **2**. Draw two diagonal lines that connect the opposite corners of the square **3**.

To the right and left of the square will be the pattern inside the thin rectangles with repeating triangles for multi-level carving. Mark dots 1.5cm from the outer side of the rectangle, above and below **4**, then connect them **5**. Repeat this on the other side.

Next, draw a circle inside the main square with a radius of 5.1cm **6**.

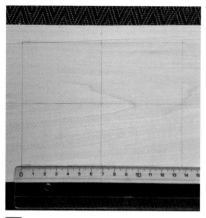

1 Draw a rectangle 13.7cm long and 10.2cm wide, then draw two intersecting perpendicular lines.

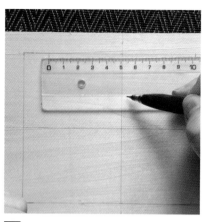

2 Mark dots 5.1cm from the vertical perpendicular line.

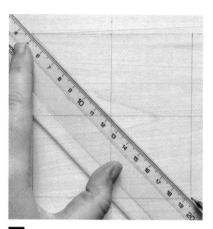

3 Draw diagonal lines inside the central square.

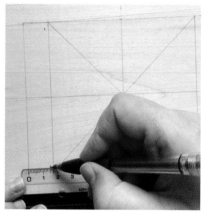

4 Mark dots 1.5cm from the outer side of the rectangle.

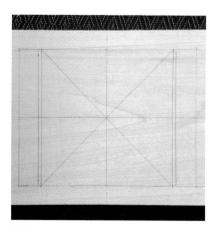

5 Connect the dots.

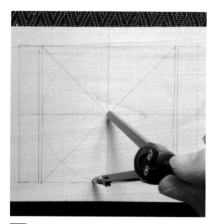

6 Using a compass, draw a circle with a radius of 5.1cm inside the central square.

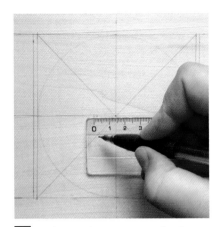

7 Mark two dots 1.4cm and 1.2cm for drawing two more circles.

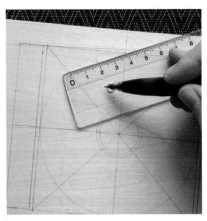

8 Divide the sections of the circle in half.

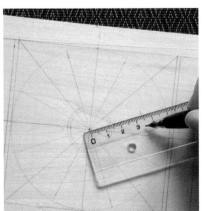

9 Draw the central lines inside the sections.

10 Mark dots 3.4cm from the centre on the central lines of the sections.

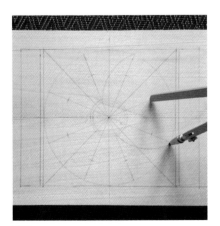

11 Place a compass on one of the dots and draw curved lines to the right and left of it.

12 Repeat this on the other dots.

Inside this circle, draw two more, with radiuses of 1.4cm and 1.2cm **7**.

Divide all eight sections of the main circle in half **8** and draw lines connected at the centre **9**. On the resulting lines, mark dots 3.4cm from the centre of the pattern **10**. Place a compass on one of the dots and draw curved lines to the right and left of it, starting from the second circle and ending at the line of the main circle **11**. Repeat these steps on the remaining dots, each time drawing two lines from one dot **12**. The main 'petals' for the central main pattern are done. You still need to divide them into separate triangles for carving, but you will do that later.

Now, mark a dot 4mm from the outer circle **13**. Position a compass on the centre of the pattern and draw curved lines between the petals.

Next, you need to delimit the space between the petals. To do this, on the recently drawn curved lines, mark dots 4.5mm to the left and right of the perpendicular and diagonal lines **14**. Connect those points where the central perpendicular and diagonal lines intersect the main circle with the resulting dots **15**. Then, by hand, draw curved lines from the same two dots down to where the petals intersect each other **16**.

The following steps that need to be done to completely delimit the space between the petals are to divide the two halves of the space in half. Connect the resulting dot on one side with the two previously prepared, and on the other with the dot where the prepared curved line crosses the petal **17**, **18**.

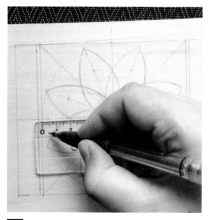

13 Mark a dot 4mm from the outer circle then place a compass on the centre of the pattern and draw curved lines between the petals.

14 Mark dots 4.5mm to the left and right of the perpendicular and diagonal lines.

15 Connect the dots with the points where the perpendicular lines intersect the main circle.

16 Draw curved lines from the dots down to where the petals intersect each other.

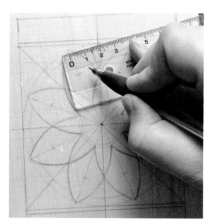

17 Divide the space between the petals in half.

18 Connect the dots with the places where the curved line intersects the petals.

19 Repeat these steps in all the spaces between the petals.

20 Start marking dots inside the petals; mark the first one 9mm from the top.

Repeat these steps in all the spaces between the petals **19**.

Next, start filling the petals with the following lines: first, mark a dot 9mm from its top on one side **20**, and the next dot 8mm from the first one **21**. Starting from them, draw curved lines by hand; these will connect where the lower lines of the petal are connected to each other **22**. Repeat these steps on the other side, and then in the remaining petals **23**.

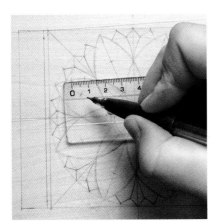

21 Mark the next dot 8mm from the first one.

22 Connect the dots at the point where the bottom lines of the petals connect with each other.

23 Repeat this inside each petal.

An interesting detail of the entire pattern is a slightly different filling for carving in the petals, which is repeated inside every other one. Start with the petal second from the vertical perpendicular line to the left. Mark a dot 1.2cm from the top of the petal, on its central line . Then, to draw a rhombus at the top and a triangle without a base at the bottom, draw two lines to connect this dot with the beginning of the line that is closer to the central line of the petal .

Connect the corners of the rhombus together **26**. Repeat these steps in every other petal **27**.

Inside those triangles formed by intersecting petals, it is necessary to draw one more triangle for multi-level chips. To do this, mark a dot 2.2cm on their central lines from the centre of the pattern **28**. Then connect them to the bases of triangles **29**.

24 Mark a dot 1.2cm from the top of the petal, on its central line.

25 Connect the dot with the first lines inside the petal.

26 Connect the corners of the rhombus together.

27 Repeat this inside every other petal.

28 Mark a dot 2.2cm from the centre of the pattern on the central line in the triangle around the central pattern.

29 Connect the dot with the triangle's base.

30 Mark a dot 5mm from the centre.

31 Draw a circle with a 5mm radius.

To draw a star in the centre of the pattern, step 5mm away from the centre **30** and draw a circle with a 5mm radius **31**. Now mark dots on every other line, starting with one to the left of the central perpendicular line **32**. Connect them together wherever a line without a dot intersects the inner circle **33**, **34**.

32 Mark dots on every other line, starting with one to the left of the central perpendicular line.

33 Connect the dots with the points where a line without a dot intersects the inner circle.

34 The drawn central pattern.

In the main pattern, you now need to draw patterns in the corners. To do this, step 1.6cm away from the corners of the square to the right and left, up and down **35**. Place a compass on this point and draw a curved line with a 1.6cm radius, starting from the corner of the square to the outer circle **36**. Repeat this on the remaining dots **37**.

Next, connect the dots from each corner together, but draw lines only inside the ovals to divide the resulting ovals in half **38**. Step 3mm away from the sides of the ovals **39**. Again, by placing a compass on the dots on the sides of the square, draw curved lines on both sides **40**.

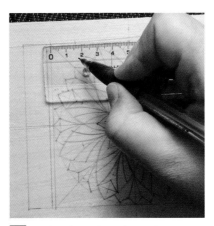

35 Mark a dot 1.6cm from the corners of the square.

36 Place the compass on the dot and draw a curved line.

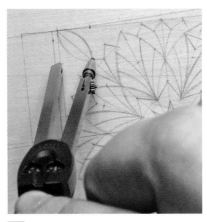

37 Place the compass on the other dots and draw another curved line.

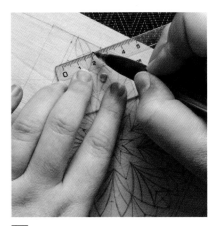

38 Draw the central line inside the oval that divides it into two triangles connected by bases.

39 Mark a dot 3mm from the side of the oval.

40 Place the compass on the dots on the sides of the square and draw curved lines on both sides of the oval.

41 Mark a dot 3mm from the side of the oval.

42 Draw curved lines using a compass, placing it on the centre of the pattern.

Next, step 3mm from the outer circle **41**, place a compass on the centre of the pattern and draw curved lines **42**, **43**.

Now draw the thin rectangles to the right and left of the square. Start from the inside line, marking dots at 1cm intervals along it. Where there is a central line, mark dots 5mm to the right and left of it, equal to half the size of the triangle's base **44**.

On the outside line, mark dots at 1cm intervals, but starting right from the central line **45**. Connect the dots as shown in picture **46**.

43 The pattern inside the central square is completely drawn.

44 Mark dots 5mm to the right and left from the central line, equal to half the size of the triangle's base.

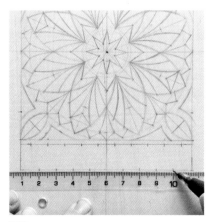

45 Mark the dots on the outer side of the rectangle.

46 Connect the dots together.

Here are the completed triangles **47**. Now draw the thickness of the resulting lines. To do this, from each line of the triangles, mark dots 1mm to the right and left and draw lines parallel to the sides of the triangles **48**, **49**. Repeat these steps on the other side.

The pattern is now ready for carving **50**.

47 The completed triangles.

48 Mark dots 1mm to the right and left of each line of the triangles.

CARVING PROCESS

Here I will show you how to carve the entire pattern by demonstrating just one quarter. This pattern combines: carving against the grain, carving along the grain and carving in different directions.

Start carving the pattern from the petal that is closer to the horizontal perpendicular line. Undercutting the facets of the triangles in this pattern is done at 45 degrees, while cutting the sides of the straight-wall chips and multi-level chips is done at almost 90 degrees.

There are four triangles that are separated from each other by non-cutting spaces – two triangles on one side and two triangles on the other one, joined to each other by facets. In the first petal, it is easy to see what to carve first: one chip is smaller in size/length; the other is bigger. First, carve the smaller triangle **51**, **52**, then the one that covers the first. The side of the second chip, which is

49 Draw lines parallel to the sides of the triangles.

50 The pattern is drawn.

51 Carve the first triangle in the first petal at an angle of 45 degrees.

52 The first triangle carved.

53 Carve the second triangle of the first petal by changing the knife grip when necessary.

54 The second triangle is carved.

closer to the non-cutting space, is slightly rounded to the top of the chip itself. Therefore, it is in this rounded area that you will need to change the knife grip when undercutting **53**, **54**.

When the first two triangles are ready, carve the other two in this petal, following the same steps **55**. Start cutting the straight-wall chips, connected to each other by the bases **56**. The bottom one is simple, but to carve the top one you will need to carve one more chip inside it **57**.

Next, carve the second petal in this quarter of the pattern. There are no more non-cutting spaces, and all the chips are connected with each other. In this case, it is better to start carving with those triangles that are near and that are connected by facets **58**.

55 Carve another two triangles in the first petal, following the sequence of steps.

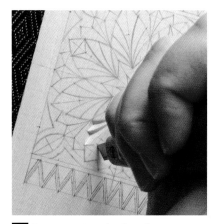

56 Start cutting the first bottom straight-wall chips.

57 Carve the top straight-wall chip and then one more chip inside it.

58 Start carving the second petal with the triangles that are connected by facets.

Next, cut those triangles to the left and right of the newly cut-out triangles, first on one side **59**, **60** then on the other **61**.

Between these two petals there are three elongated rhombuses that are connected to each other. To identify them on the wood, you must first cut the straight-wall chips, which run around the perimeter of the circle between the rhombuses **62**, and then the lines between the rhombuses. Put the knife 1mm from each line by eye and make undercuts to the right and left of them at an angle of 60 degrees **63**, **64**.

59 Carve the triangles to the left of the first carved one.

60 The triangles are carved.

61 Now carve the triangles on the other side.

62 Carve the straight-wall chips that run around the perimeter of the circle between the rhombuses.

63 Make undercuts to the right and left of the lines between the rhombuses at 60 degrees.

64 The undercuts are complete.

65 Push the knife tip at the deepest place of the intersecting corners of the chip, at an angle of almost 90 degrees.

66 Lead the knife to the base of the triangle.

67 Carve the chip by putting the bevel of the knife parallel to the side where the undercut is going.

68 Carve a smaller chip inside the big one.

69 Carve another straight-wall chip on the other side of the corner pattern and a small chip inside it.

Then carve the straight-wall chips around the pattern in the corner of the square. Since they are big, you will not be able to do this simply by pushing the tip of the knife in the deepest place and lowering the heel. To make the cut, place the knife tip in the deepest place **65**, and lead the knife almost at 90 degrees to the base of the triangle using the tip of the knife **66**. Repeat this on the other side of the straight-wall chip, then carve the chip by putting the bevel of the knife parallel to the side where the undercutting is going **67**. Next, carve another chip inside this big one **68**, and then another big straight-wall chip on the other side of the corner pattern and a small chip inside it **69**. Since the undercutting of the second multi-level chip goes along the grain, carefully check when the knife smoothly goes through the grain.

Now start carving a corner pattern, where two chips with curved sides are connected to each other by bases. The cut of these chips is the same as for the previous big ones, but here the tip of the knife gently goes along the curved sides **70**. Carve this **71** and the opposite chip, following the direction of the grain when undercutting **72**. Then carve the smaller chips inside them **73**.

Next, start carving the straight-wall chips around the central pattern, and then the smaller ones inside them **74**.

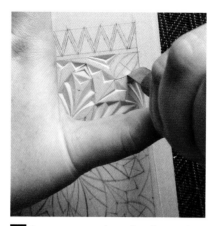

70 Start cutting the side of one of the chips inside the oval.

71 Then carve it.

72 Carve the second chip inside the oval.

73 Carve the smaller chips inside the chips.

74 Start carving the straight-wall chips around the central pattern.

75 When undercutting the curved chip, which goes along the grain away from you, position the knife a little to the left beyond the line.

76 When undercutting towards yourself, position the knife a little to the right beyond the central line.

The chip that goes along the grain has a slightly rounded base that cannot be undercut with one movement towards you or away from you. Therefore, when undercutting, go a little beyond the central line; namely, when undercutting away from you, put the knife a little to the left beyond the central line **75**, and when undercutting towards yourself put the knife a little to the right **76**. You need to begin to cut from the very curved part. Now carve the smaller chips inside them **77**, then the straight-wall chips around the star **78**. Now cut the straight-wall chips inside the thin rectangle to the left of the square. Carve them out **79** and then the other small chips inside them **80**.

The first quarter of the pattern is carved; now carve the other three quarters of the design **81**.

77 Three straight-wall multi-level chips around the central circle are done.

78 Start carving the chips between the rays of the central star.

79 Start carving the chips inside the thin rectangle.

80 Then carve the smaller chips inside them.

81 The carving is now complete.

SUNFLOWER

For the final pattern, I tried to choose one that would combine everything you have learned to do, starting with simple patterns like straight-wall chips and line carving to two-sided chips and multi-level carving.

TOOLS AND MATERIALS

- BASSWOOD BOARD (AT LEAST 100–120MM SQUARE AND 15MM THICK)

- 0.5MM MECHANICAL PENCIL WITH H OR HB LEAD

- RULER

- COMPASS

- SKEW KNIFE

- SANDPAPER OR LEATHER STRIPS FOR SHARPENING

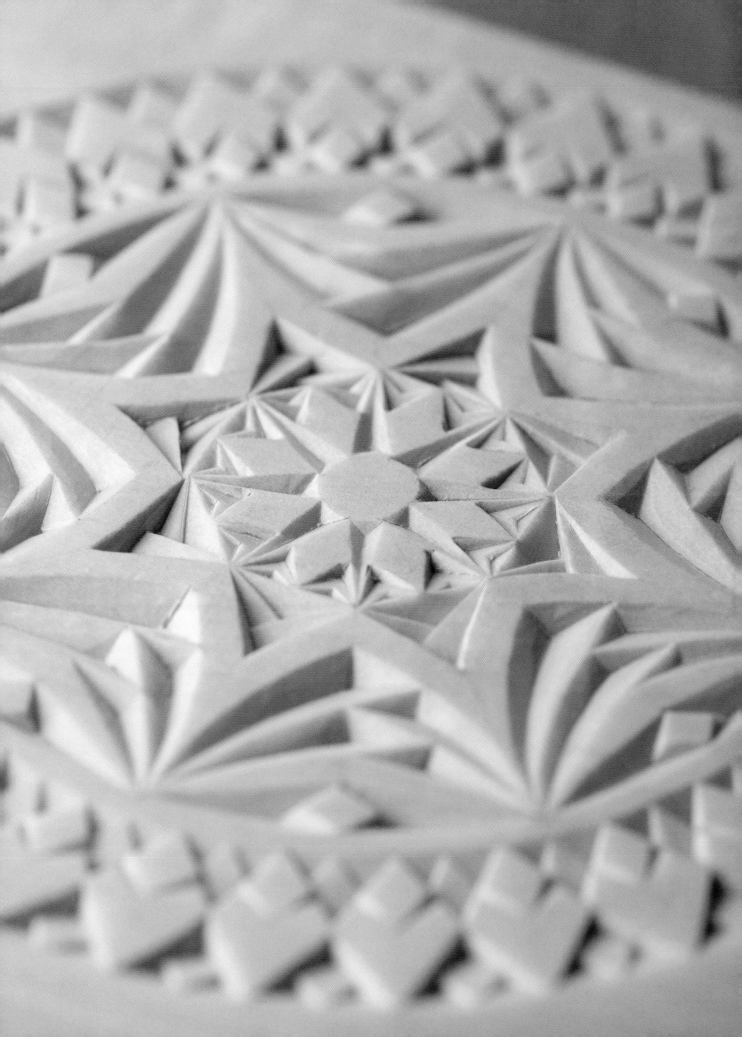

DRAWING PROCESS

If you would prefer to transfer this pattern to the basswood board, the template is on page 171, and guidelines on page 12. Otherwise, if you prefer to draw the pattern directly on to the basswood board, follow the instructions below.

First draw a square with the sides 13.2cm long. Then draw two perpendicular lines that intersect at the centre and two diagonal lines that connect the opposite corners of the square. Next, prepare a circle for the central and main pattern. Using a compass, draw a circle with a radius of 6.6cm inside the square **1**. On one of the perpendicular lines, mark two dots, 1.8cm and 2cm from the edge of the circle **2**. Placing a compass on the centre of the pattern, draw two more circles **3**.

Next, divide all sections of the main circle in half **4** and draw the central lines.

Measure a radius of 4.7cm and, placing the compass on the dot where the vertical perpendicular line intersects the outer circle, draw a curved line in the left section of this line to the left of its central line **5**. Then put the compass on the dot where the diagonal line intersects the outer circle – that is, on every other line from the previous one – and draw a similar curved line **6**.

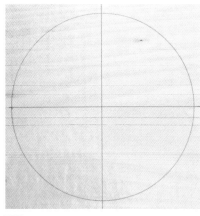

1 Draw a square with 13.2cm-long sides and draw a 6.6cm-radius circle inside it.

2 Mark two dots 1.8cm and 2cm from the edge of the circle.

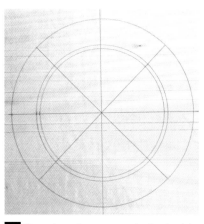

3 Now draw two more circles inside the first one.

4 Divide the sections of the circle in half and draw the central lines.

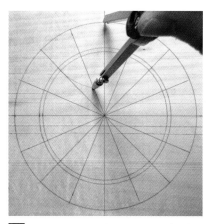

5 Draw a curved line to the left of the central line.

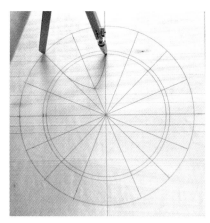

6 Draw another curved line to the right of the central line.

7 Draw two more curved lines in the next section.

8 Measure a radius of 5.1cm and, placing a compass on the dots, draw curved lines repeating the contours of the main shapes.

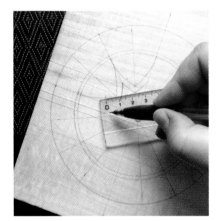

9 Mark a dot 8mm from the top on the side to the left of the central line of the section.

10 Connect the dots with the base on the opposite sides.

Repeat these steps to draw the same shape in the next section of the circle, on the left **7**. Next, measure a radius of 5.1cm and, putting the compass on the same dots, draw the curved lines again **8**.

Now begin to fill inside the previously drawn shapes with triangles that will cover one another. First, inside one shape, mark a first dot 8mm from the top, on the side that goes to the left of the central line of the section in which this shape is located, and then in the next section **9**. Connect the resulting points with the base on the opposite side of the figure with a line that follows the contours of the side **10**. If you find this difficult, try the method described in the panel below.

METHOD FOR DRAWING A SMOOTH CURVED LINE

Place your little finger at a comfortable distance from the drawn line, put the tip of the pencil on the starting point and start leading the pencil to the end point, moving it smoothly with the other four fingers while the little finger remains in place.

Draw the next line from the base of the opposite line to the point where the previous line intersects the centre of the figure **11**; that is, the previous triangle that covers this one.

Next, mark a dot 8mm on the long side of the resulting triangle from the central line **12**, and connect it to the base of the opposite side **13**. Repeat the steps with the next line **14**.

Now mark a dot 3mm from the dot on the central line where the long side of the last lower triangle intersects it **15**. Connect this with straight lines to the base of this shape/triangle **16**.

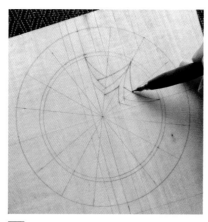

11 Draw a line from the base of the opposite line to the point where the previous line intersects the centre of the figure.

12 Mark a dot 8mm on the long side of the triangle from the central line.

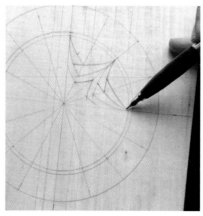

13 Connect the dot to the base of the opposite side.

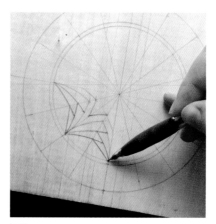

14 Draw the next line.

15 Mark a dot 3mm from the point on the central line where the long side of the last lower triangle intersects it.

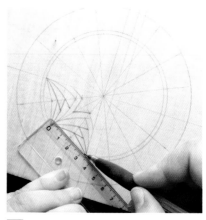

16 Connect a dot to the base of the shape with straight lines.

17 Connect up the opposite dots.

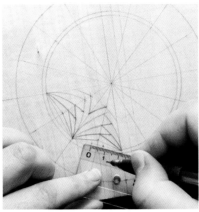

18 Mark dots 4mm on the line, to the right and left of the central line of the shape.

Inside the resulting triangle, connect the opposite dots together **17** and mark dots 4mm on this line, to the right and left of the central line of the shape **18**. Connect these points together to form a rhombus **19**.

Now begin to draw the space that is formed by the outer circle and the circle that follows from it. Divide each small rectangle in half **20**. Then, by connecting this dot with the centre of the pattern using a ruler, draw lines in these rectangles **21**.

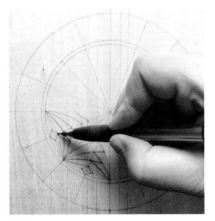

19 Connect the dots as a rhombus.

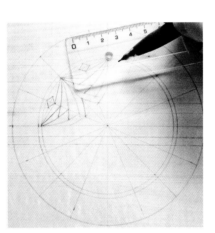

20 Divide each small rectangle in half.

21 Draw lines in the rectangles, using a ruler to connect the dot with the centre of the pattern.

Next, divide the space between the outer and the next circle in half  and draw another circle using a compass 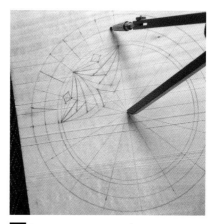.

Divide the small rectangle in half once again 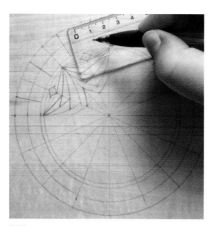 and draw lines in the previously divided rectangles – this line will be central in the future rhombuses . Draw rhombuses 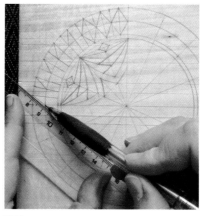.

Mark a dot 5mm from the second circle .

22 Divide the space between the outer and the second circle in half.

23 Draw one more circle using a compass.

24 Divide the small rectangle in half once again.

25 Draw the central lines inside the rectangle.

26 Now draw rhombuses inside the rectangle.

27 Now mark a dot 5mm from the second circle.

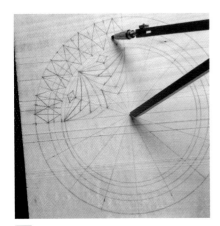

28 Draw a circle using a compass.

29 Draw short lines from the centre of the rhombus, right and left, to the dots where the circle crosses the bottom sides of the rhombuses.

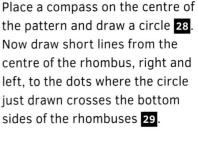

Place a compass on the centre of the pattern and draw a circle **28**. Now draw short lines from the centre of the rhombus, right and left, to the dots where the circle just drawn crosses the bottom sides of the rhombuses **29**.

If you have not drawn directly inside the remaining quarter of the circle, then repeat all the steps and complete them. In order to finish drawing the pattern in the centre, it is necessary for the rest of the pattern to be drawn first **30**.

Start connecting the apexes of the lines that follow the contours of the main shapes/triangles of the pattern **31**. Then mark a dot 5mm from the centre on one of the central lines **32** and draw a circle using a compass **33**.

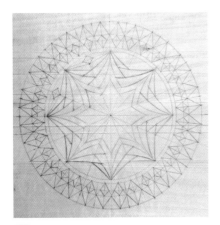

30 Finish filling the other sections of the circle with the patterns.

31 Start connecting together the apexes of the lines that follow the contours of the main shapes.

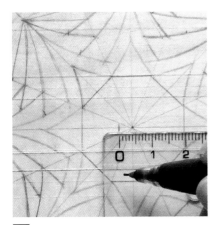

32 Mark a dot 5mm from the centre on one of the central lines.

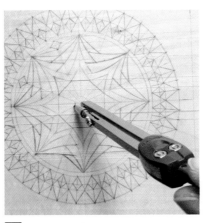

33 Draw a circle using a compass.

Mark dots using a pencil, starting where the vertical perpendicular line intersects the circle you have just drawn. Mark them on every other line **34**. Draw a star **35**. Next, mark a dot 1cm from the centre of the pattern **36** and draw short lines using a compass **37**. Connect the dots in the middle of the base of the triangle with those points where the previously drawn short lines intersect the sides of the rays of the star **38**.

The pattern is now ready for carving **39**.

34 Mark dots on every other line, starting where the vertical perpendicular line intersects the circle you have just drawn.

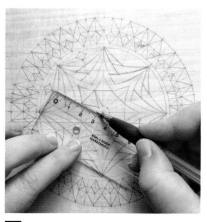

35 Draw a star, connecting the dots with the bases of the triangles.

36 Mark a dot 1cm from the centre of the pattern.

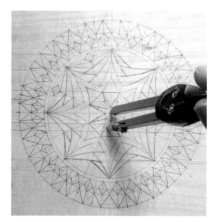

37 Draw short lines by using a compass on every ray of the star.

38 Connect the dots with the central line of the triangle at their bases.

39 The pattern is drawn.

CARVING PROCESS

Here I will show you how to carve the entire pattern by demonstrating just the top left quarter of the pattern. This pattern combines (like all the other quarters): a) carving against the grain, b) carving along the grain and c) carving in different directions.

Begin the pattern by carving a big triangle with curved sides close to the vertical perpendicular line. Carve the lower triangle in this shape first, holding the knife at a 45-degree angle when undercutting all sides **40**. Carve out the remaining triangles, which overlap each other **41**.

Next, go to the base of this shape and start to cut the rhombus **42**. Then cut the sides of the triangle without a base, first one, and then the opposite one **43**, **44**.

Now, move to the next big triangle and carve it, following the steps as for the previous shape **45**.

40 Carve the lower triangle in the first shape, holding the knife at a 45-degree angle.

41 Carve out the remaining triangles.

42 Undercut the sides of the rhombus.

43 Carve the sides of the triangles without bases.

44 The first section is done.

45 Two carved sections are complete.

Next, work on the small straight-wall chips in the central pattern. These need to be carved before you can work on the big straight-wall chips around the central pattern **46**. Cut a large triangle that connects with the bases of the small triangles **47**, then start carving other chips inside the small ones, working carefully with only the knife tip **48**.

Inside the big chips you will need to carve two chips; one of these needs to go clockwise and the other anticlockwise. Cut the first chip, starting from the right side of the big triangle, step about 3mm from the top by eye **49**. Then cut the side of the big triangle itself again, starting from where the previous undercut begins, and carve the smaller chip **50**.

Make the first cut for the next small straight-wall chip to the left side of the recently carved chip; that is, anticlockwise **51**.

46 Carve the small straight-wall chips in the central pattern first.

47 Then carve the big straight-wall chip that connects with the bases of the small triangles.

48 Start carving other chips inside the small ones, carefully working only with the tip of the knife.

49 Cut the first chip, starting from the right side of the big triangle, stepping about 3mm from the top.

50 Carve the first small chip inside the big one.

51 Start cutting the second small chip from the left side of the first small chip.

52 Undercut the side of the first small chip one more time.

53 Then carve the second small chip.

54 The first chain of chips is done.

55 Carve the remaining chain of chips.

56 Gently touch the apex of the triangle with the tip of the knife, holding the knife at a 45-degree angle.

57 Rotate the board and begin to undercut the other side of the triangle, following the direction of the grain.

Then cut the side of the previous chip again **52** and carve this second small straight-wall chip **53**. When the first chain of chips is done **54**, carve the next chain, following the same steps, starting with the small chips and ending with the big ones **55**.

The next stage of carving out the central pattern is the equilateral triangles located between the non-cutting rhombuses inside the central circle. You will need a sharp knife for this, so strop it on leather or abrasive strips (see page 10). Then proceed to carving. Since the tip of the triangle is very sharp and the distance between its faces is small, first hold the knife at a 45-degree angle, then gently touch the apex of the triangle with the tip of the knife **56** and begin cutting with the tip, bringing it to the base of the triangle.

Next, undercut the base, then rotate the board, and begin to undercut the other side of the triangle, following the direction of the grain **57**.

Then carve the second triangle in this quarter of the pattern **58**.

Now carve the rhombuses that go around the central large circle. Carve the first two chips that are closer to the horizontal perpendicular line. Inside these chips, above and below, you need to carve two more small chips, which will form rhombuses. Begin to cut the sides of the straight-wall chip inside the top chip: step approximately 3–4mm from the top of the chip, make a cut that ends in the middle of the big chip **59**, then make another cut on the opposite side **60**, and two more **61**, **62**. Carve these two resulting chips **63**.

58 Now carve out the second small long triangle.

59 Approximately 3–4mm from the top of the chip, make a cut that ends in the middle of the big chip.

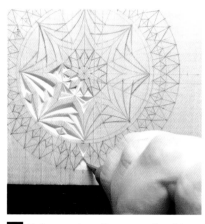

60 Make a cut on the opposite side.

61 Make two more cuts.

62 Make a further two more cuts.

63 Carve the chips.

64 Undercut the sides of the chips inside the lower big chip.

65 Carve the chips.

Now repeat these steps on the lower chip **64**, and carve the two small straight-wall chips **65**, **66**.

Next, carve the lines on the big non-cutting rhombuses below. To do this, put the knife about 1mm from the line on one side of it and then the other, and make cuts, carefully leading the knife to the place where the two lines connect **67**. When this is done **68**, carve out all the remaining rhombuses, big chips, and the rhombuses inside them **69**.

The first quarter of the pattern is complete. Now carve the remaining three quarters of the design.

The carving is now complete **70**.

66 The first multi-level chips around the central patterns are done.

67 Position the knife about 1mm from the line on one side of it and make a cut.

68 Carve the lines completely.

69 Carve out all the remaining rhombuses, big chips and rhombuses inside them.

70 The carving is now complete.

TEMPLATES

PRACTICE BOARD SIDE 1

PRACTICE BOARD SIDE 2

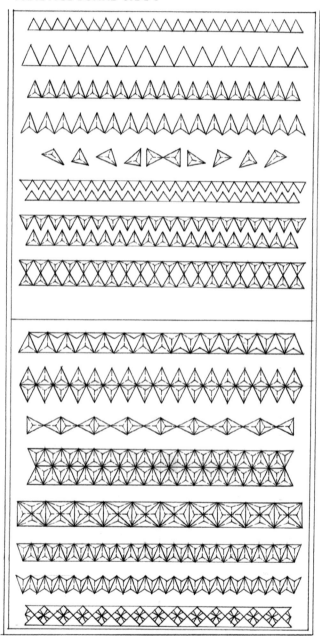

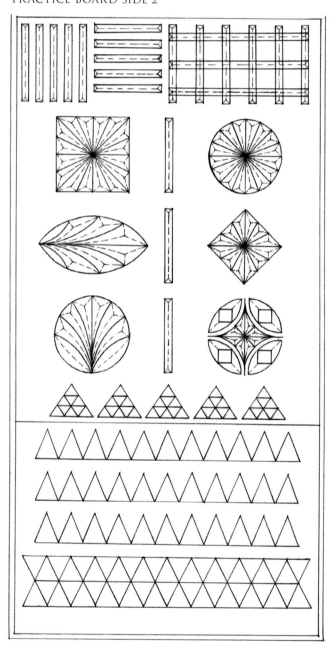

TEMPLATE SIZES

All templates are shown at 100% size except the practice boards,
which need to be enlarged on a photocopier at 150%. See page 12 for
how to transfer them to your basswood board.

PATTERN 1

PATTERN 2

PATTERN 3

PATTERN 4

PATTERN 5

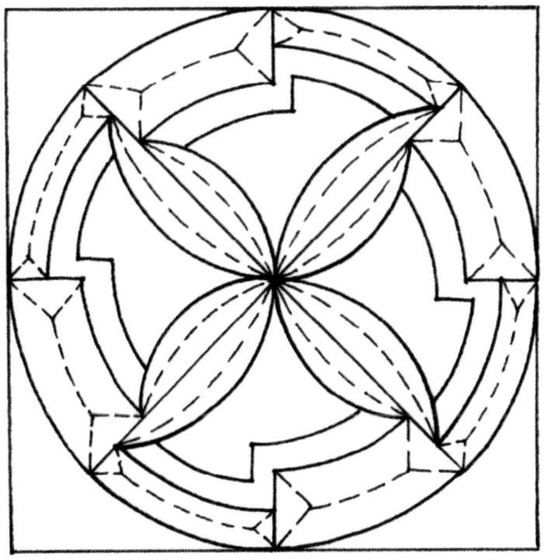

PATTERN 6

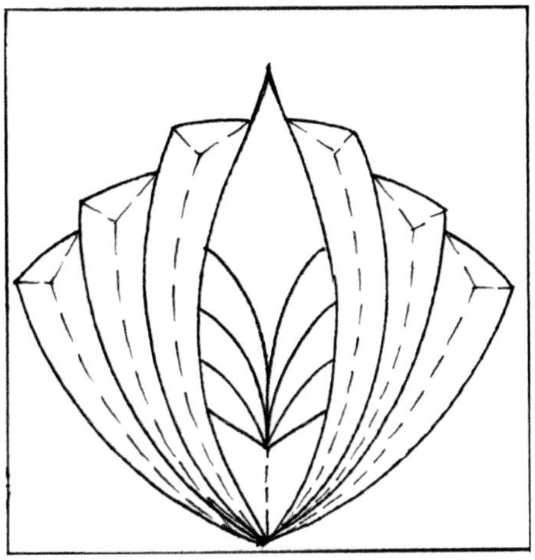

PATTERN 7

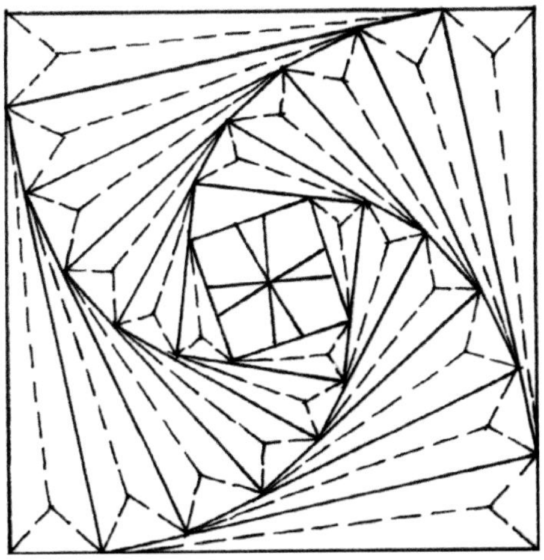

PATTERN 8

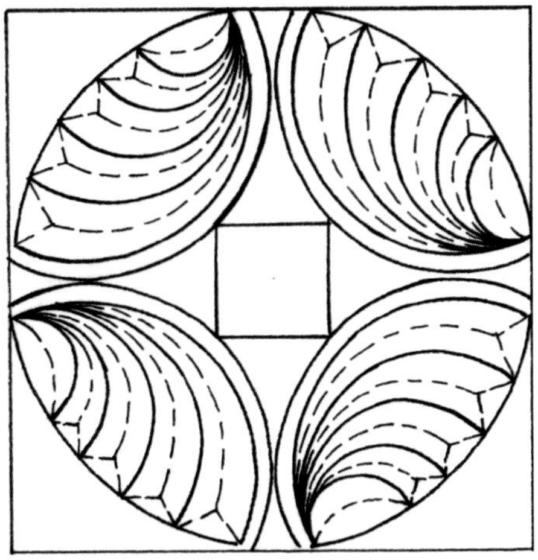

PATTERN 9

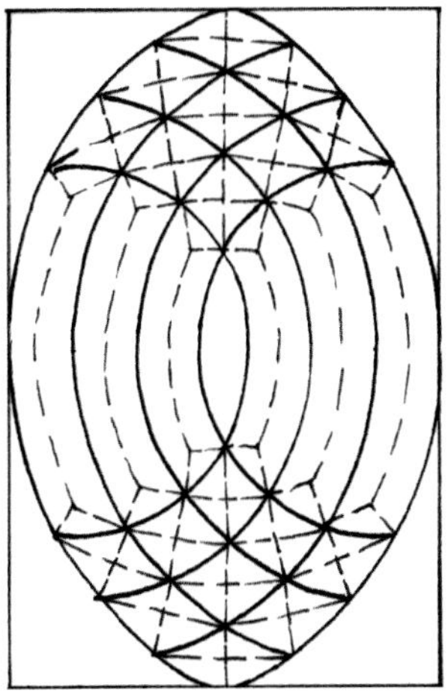

PATTERN 10

PATTERN 11

PATTERN 12

PATTERN 13

PATTERN 14

Gallery

These examples show how chip carving is used to decorate three-dimensional objects. These pieces are made from basswood and finished with Danish oil (apart from the round box, bottom left). The hexagon box (below) is dedicated to St. Petersburg, Russia and every detail has a meaning linked to the city.

The rounded box (left), was inspired by the Earth, stars and galaxies. The box is made out of basswood, covered with milk paint before carving, then finished with amber varnish.

The rectangular box (above) is inspired by my grandfather's wooden house, where the central pattern is a wooden window and the leaves represent a garden.

The coaster (left) is inspired by the moment before a sunset, with a swirl that runs through the pattern, covered in gold leaf.

INDEX

ABOUT THE AUTHOR

Tatiana Baldina is a professional woodcarving artist who lives and works in Russia. She specializes in chip carving and chose to study the subject as part of her Applied Fine Arts degree at the Volga Regional State University. After graduating, Tatiana went on to create many of her own original pieces; she also worked for several companies producing carved boxes and other items for the home. Tatiana is a Laureate of The International Association of the Creative Professions, Vatikam, France. She has worked as a freelance woodcarver since 2014.

Follow on Instagram: @tatbalcarvings
Show us your chip carving using the hashtag #chipcarving

First published 2019 by Guild of Master Craftsman Publications Ltd
Castle Place, 166 High Street, Lewes, East Sussex, BN7 1XU, UK

Text © Tatiana Baldina, 2019

Copyright in the Work © GMC Publications Ltd, 2019

ISBN 978 1 78494 546 6

While every effort has been made to obtain permission from the copyright holders for all material used in this book, the publishers will be pleased to hear from anyone who has not been appropriately acknowledged and to make the correction in future reprints.

The publishers and author can accept no legal responsibility for any consequences arising from the application of information, advice or instructions given in this publication.

A catalogue record for this book is available from the British Library.

Publisher Jonathan Bailey
Production Jim Bulley and Jo Pallett
Senior Project Editor Virginia Brehaut
Editor Nicola Hodgson
Managing Art Editor Gilda Pacitti
Art Editor Cathy Challinor
Main photography Andrew Perris
Step-by-step photography Tatiana Baldina

Colour origination by GMC Reprographics
Printed and bound in China

To place an order or to request
a catalogue, contact:

GMC Publications Ltd, Castle Place, 166 High
Street, Lewes, East Sussex, BN7 1XU United
Kingdom
Tel: +44 (0)1273 488005

www.gmcbooks.com

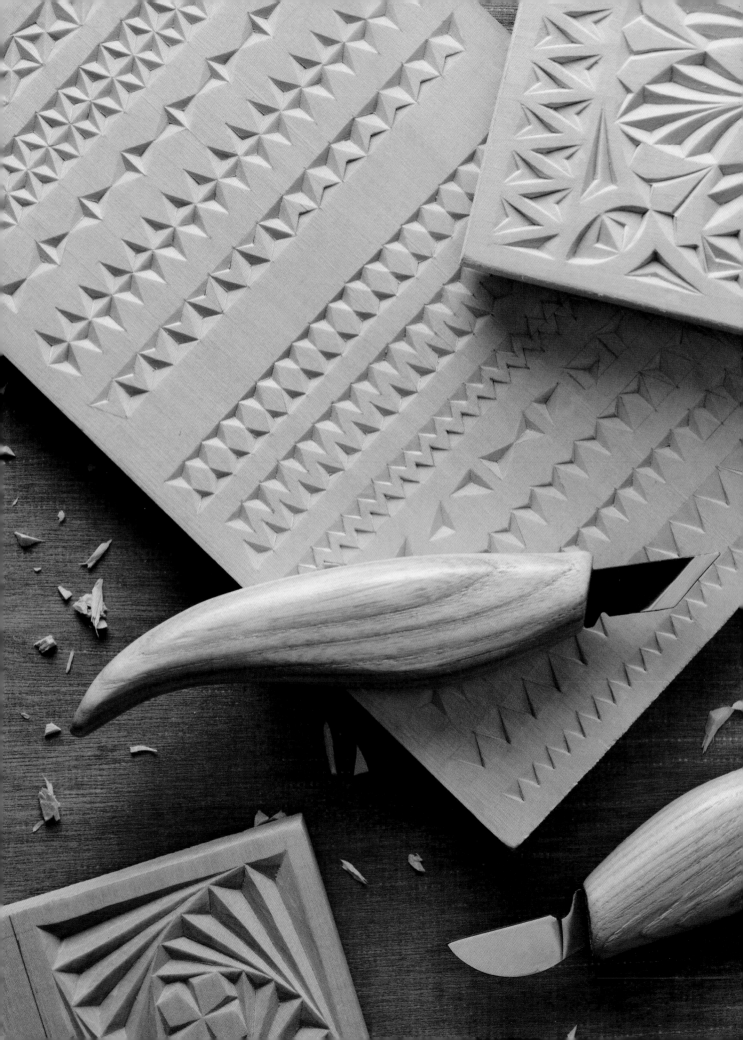